HOW TO
Catch Fairies

GILLY SERGIEV

*The Beauty and Fertility in Nature
is a reflection of Fairy Work.
To Elizabeth and Michael Fenn
and to all these Fairies and Wild Things I say:
"Come dance with me, for I am the Gana Chovhani."*

FAIR WINDS
PRESS
GLOUCESTER, MASSACHUSETTS

Text © 2002 by Gilly Sergiev

First published in in the United States of America in 2002 by
Fair Winds Press
33 Commercial Street
Gloucester, MA 01930

Designed for Fair Winds Press by The Bridgewater Book Company

Illustrations on pages 53, 55, 57, 59, 63, 67, 71, 73, 75, 77, 81, 83, 87, 91, 93, 95, 97, 99,103, 105, 107, 111, 113, 114, 119, 120, 123, 127 by Ivan Hissey

10 9 8 7 6 5 4 3 2 1

Printed and bound in China

ISBN 1–931412-21-9

The publishers would like to thank the following libraries for permission to reproduce copyright material:
BRIDGEMAN ART LIBRARY p9. CAMERON COLLECTION pp2, 10, 15, 19, 26, 29, 30, 33, 36, 38, 40, 43, 45, 49, 61, 64, 100, 125. GLASGOW MUSEUMS AND ART GALLERY p41; GUILDHALL ART GALLERY, CORPORATION OF LONDON p35, 39; PRIVATE COLLECTION p50; THE DE MORGAN FOUNDATION p28.

more than others, it is true), but there is far more to fairies than mere amusement. Apart from their magickal talents of dance and music, which bring lightness to our world, they also have a deeply serious role to play in our lives. Fairies can teach us the secrets of the Otherworld, the ancient secrets of old that empower and help us with our struggles in this world. However, fairies often debate the relevance of passing on their sacred knowledge. Most humans scorn their existence and so it is only to those who believe in the fairy realms that fairies appear.

The uncertainty of human belief—whether we are really ready to listen—is the main problem that fairies face. Fairies want to coexist with us, but every time we deny a belief in them, we are making their existence harder. So, never say you don't believe in fairies and you will be on the path to a wonderful and most secret world.

The fairies are just waiting for your call; and once you have a fairy friend, you can be sure that you are blessed indeed. If a fairy plays a trick on you, he or she is usually trying to draw your attention to or teach you something. For example, I recently had a gold earring taken by a house brownie. I searched high and low, but there was no sign of my earring anywhere. Eventually, at dusk, I called out to the fairies and asked for it to be returned. After a while, I heard a tiny noise behind me, and as I turned around, there on the floor lay my earring. You couldn't have missed it even if you'd tried. It was lying in the middle of the room, as if the brownie had

put it there for all the world to see. When I picked it up (thanking the brownie), I noticed that its butterfly back was missing. By taking it and then placing it in my path, the brownie had shown me that without the butterfly I was in danger of losing my earring for good.

Once you have discovered the way to find and keep fairies in your life, the magick never stops. You will see them everywhere and in everything, and once they know you can see them, they will never leave you—fairies will become your family.

The whole reason to catch a fairy is when you are in need of its enchantments for some reason or another. You should never try to keep fairies against their will, because they will stay around only those who love and respect them. If a fairy is unhappy, not only is it harder to find (it tends to fade or stay in dark corners), but its mood affects your home or surroundings. If lightbulbs keep blowing, or the cat goes missing, you can be fairly certain that your fairy is unhappy. Ultimately, fairies will always evade capture if they really want to: in their pure form they are beings of ethereal light, able to slip through any bindings. It is your responsibility to treat them so well that they will be reluctant to escape.

When I was a little girl, the family would often travel in our big old car to visit my grandmother. On these seemingly interminable journeys, I would look out of the window, and as we drew nearer to her house, I would start to see my tree fairies. It always brought me a feeling of such happiness that I'm amazed I never told anyone at the time. Seeing those tree spirits seemed as normal to me as spotting the friendly faces of the girls who served in the shop where we always stopped. First I would see a tree, and then, almost as if it were an afterthought, I would see the spirit of the tree as we flashed past in the car. Once

spindly alders showing their urchin faces, and strong, full oak trees with ancient, wise faces. Old, young, middle-aged spirits—I saw them all. And the fairies saw me. From that moment, we held a deep connection between us, and since the time when I saw my first dryads (and that was many years ago now), my knowledge has increased and I seem able to see myriad fairies wherever I go.

I have a particularly amusing group of gnomes who inhabit my bathroom and a dear little hearthfay who is constantly finding things I have lost and hopping about, radiating love wherever she goes. I've never looked directly at my hearthfay visitor, but I see her from the corner of my eye when she chooses to rush past on one of her many errands. All movements that she makes are in a hurried manner, and I usually see a dark little blur hopping about.

Once, she rushed past my foot

I was on that level, I began to look in advance for the trees. Although the car was traveling reasonably fast, the fairy world on the other side of the window was slowed down and constant, so I could look as much as I liked. The tree spirits would be everywhere: I would see tall, thin garden poplars dressed as lace-embellished fops, dancing cherry trees with full skirts and blonde curling wigs, little

unexpectedly and I fell over, thinking it was my cat and trying to avoid a collision. When I pulled myself up from the floor and looked across the room, my cat simply stared at me lazily from the window ledge where she had been sleeping. Meanwhile, a candle fell over in the fireplace as my hearthfay hurriedly returned to her hiding place.

If you talk to your fairies naturally and spontaneously (perhaps even leaving them little gifts from time to time) and, most importantly, think about them, they will enter your life most willingly and bring wonders to your everyday existence. You may see them spontaneously, or this may take a little longer, but if your belief is strong and you accept their presence, you will never be alone. Once you have "caught" your fairy, it may prefer to stay invisible. However, with patience and practice not only should you acquire the knowledge of how to see them, but very often

they will spontaneously appear when you least expect it, having attuned themselves metaphysically to your home and made it theirs too. Even dear little naughty fairies have something to teach, and they are always sure to make you laugh.

There are so many different types of fairy that inhabit our worlds: they are all kinds of sizes and shapes, their habits and characters vary, they differ in magickal abilities and powers, and some are well known and others less so. In this book, I have attempted to list some of the better known ones.

If you have the good fortune to be visited by fairies, it would be useful for you to know how to look after them and keep them happy in your home. If you don't have fairies in your life—well, you could always try to catch one. This book has been written to share with you

a basic knowledge of the fairy world and to show you how wonderful it could be, having fairies in your life. Whether they visit or are caught, fairies will stay only if you treat them in the right way, so it is essential to know how to look after them and keep them happy. Good luck!

THE ORIGINS OF FAIRIES

Fairies are believed to be the original descendants of a race of magickal people, known in Britain as the Tuatha Dé Danann (people of the Goddess Danu), and humans. They lived mostly in the Tir Nau Og, or Otherworld, an enchanted land existing in a parallel universe, and separated by the flimsiest whisper of a magickal veil from the human world. With the passage of time, over many thousands of years, this veil seemed to draw shut, and the worlds separated. Gradually the fairies in the human world began returning to their invisible realm until, by the 19th century, people began to believe that fairies had died out. We know better today, but perhaps because of our lack of interest, the fairies prefer to remain invisible, living underground, at sacred sites, or protected by the veil between the worlds.

The *sidhe* or *si* (pronounced "shee"), is the ancient word for a fairy hill, and the *bean* and *fer sidhe* are the collective names for the little women and little men of the hill. *Bean sidhe* are the various types of female fairies who live in the fairy hills and *fer sidhe* are the many different male fairies who live in the fairy hills. The *bean sidhe* and *fer sidhe* have different individual names, appearances, and abilities, but they are all similar in intensity of beauty in one way or another.

FAIRYLAND

Fairyland is a place that coexists within the magickal Otherworld (a hidden place sometimes known as the Underground Country, where summer never ends). This is the esoteric ether that runs alongside our own world but in a different dimension and time frame. Fairies can pass easily between the two worlds, knowing where the doorways are and the secret magickal passwords, but as humans who have nearly forgotten the old ways, we find it harder to do so. Druids and witches who hold fast to the old ways are also known as "walkers between the worlds," reflecting the ability to pass between the two sacred frames. Secret doorways, or "curtains," are

scattered throughout the Earth, and if you
stumble upon one or know about one, you
can easily pass over and find your way into
Fairyland. But be warned: return to the
human world can be extremely difficult and
often impossible.

There are enchanted places strongly
connected to Fairyland, which are still
vaguely known about by humans, such as the
Vale of Galoche, Broceliande (a fairy wood in
Brittany, France, where it is believed that
Merlin sleeps), and Bran's Island, in the mists
of Fairyland (another fairy glen where time
stands still, and food and drink in plenty are
delivered by invisible hands). There is, of
course, Avalon, Avilion, or Afalon the Fairy
Isle, also known as the Apple Isle (*afel* is
Welsh for apple, a symbol of goddess magick,
so Avalon means the Isle of Goddess Magick).
Its exact whereabouts are often disputed.
However, a great many people believe Avalon

exists above or beneath England's
Glastonbury Tor in the separate and mystical
Otherworld dimension. So much has been
written about Glastonbury (and many tales
differ), but without doubt it holds a strange
and compelling fascination for all mystics.
The pagan Celts knew Glastonbury as Ynys
Witrin (the Island of Glass) because long
before the marshes of that place were
eventually drained, heavy flooding turned
Glastonbury into an island every winter.

Others believe the Fairy Isle lies buried
deep under the oceans of the sea around the
fabled land of Lyonness, stretching from
Land's End at the southwestern tip of Britain,
out towards the Isles of Scilly. A great fairy
city is supposed to be situated beneath the
seven great stones that mark a point seven
miles west of Land's End. There again, still
others are convinced that certain parts of
Fairyland are situated somewhere in France.

In actual fact, Fairyland itself is all around us in its mystical frame, with communities, cities, and castles lying hidden, deep down inside the many secret ancestral burial mounds and hollow hills dotted around the world. Although the doors may be well hidden, Fairyland can be found by those who truly seek it.

MERLIN

Also known as Myrddin, Taliesin, Druid, Sorcerer, Wizard, Master of Magick, Lover of Nimue, and Father of Niniane, Merlin is best known as King Arthur's counselor. Many years before Britain was inhabited by humans, the country was believed to be called Clas Myrddin, which means Myrddin's Enclosure, and Myrddin himself was worshiped as a god. Myrddin's shrine, variously reported to be made of diamonds, mist, or glass and surrounded by whitethorn flowers, was also thought to be situated at Stonehenge. That sacred site is still to this day considered to hold a powerful doorway to the Otherworld, and within its mystic circle are the sacred tools needed to gain access. Under the wide-ranging human influences and belief systems, the god Myrddin gradually became known as

LEFT *Merlin sleeps quietly,*
awaiting his magickal time
of return to this world.

the wizard Merlin, and it was in this form that he let himself walk among humans, dispensing wisdom and healing.

The last report of Merlin was when he took the Thirteen Treasures of Britain to Bardsey Island with nine attendant bards, and was thereafter lost to mortals.

There are many ongoing discussions about where Merlin can be found now. Some believe he is asleep deep within Glastonbury

BELOW *A sacred pagan
cauldron is a fairy's special
treasured possession.*

Tor, alongside Arthur and his knights, waiting for the right moment to return. Others believe he sleeps separately at Broceliande, in France. Many believe he is among us right now and that it is possible to make an ethereal connection with him. Indeed, there is a cave situated just below Tintagel Castle in Cornwall, that is known as Merlin's Cave, and it is said that he or his spiritual essence can be found here. One thing is for certain: if you call on Merlin and your call is honor bound, he will answer you.

THE THIRTEEN TREASURES

The old lunar calendar shows thirteen months in a year, and each treasure was thought by some to be connected with each lunar month. However, the magick and power attributed to each lunar treasure are of such magnitude that there can never be one "definite" list; it is ever-changing. A basic list can be drawn up, however, based on the lore of ancient Celtic Druids and Druidesses, handed down from seer to seer. The precise meaning and relevance of the treasures is something each individual has to decide for his or herself. Like a secret code, the Druids have left us images that convey more than they seem to at first sight. By choosing a treasure and meditating on its significance, enlightenment and a magickal effect of strange mystery will enter your life.

*1. The Ring of Invisibility (The Halter): a ring that makes the wearer invisible.
2. The Warrior's Ring (The Garment): a ring that changes the color of the wearer's armor.*

3. *The Magick Candelabrum (The Chariot):*
keeps alight at all times and can be extinguished
only by a magick word.

4. *Excalibur or Caliburn (The Sword):* Arthur's
magick sword.

5. *The Graal or Grail (The Cauldron):* a goblet
known as the dispenser of world peace and healer of the
waste land. Everyone who drinks from it experiences a
profound knowledge and change in their being.

6. *The Crater (The Drinking Horn):* a goblet in
which the gods mixed the creation. Everyone who
drinks from it experiences a profound inspiration and
insight into the meaning of life.

7. *Ceridwen's Cauldron or the Cauldron of Diwrnach
(The Whetstone):* bestows eternal life on all those
who touch it.

8. *The Platter of Rhydderch the Generous
(The Platter):* bestows eternal food and never empties.

9. *The Magick Staff (The Mantle):* a stick with a
ram's head and a serpent entwined about it. An image
of the god showing his secret feminine power.

10. *The Magick Spear (The Knife):* a spear that
endlessly drips magick blood, which will heal all

those who have been wounded.

11. *The Blue Cauldron of Tyrnoe (The Pan):*
The Earth Goddess Freyja's magick torque of
fertility and divination, made of enchanted gold
and silver by four dwarves.

12. *Cauldron of Tyrnoc or Dyrnawg (The
Basket),* belonging to the giant, Chief of Annwn:
a magickal cauldron that boils food for a brave
man but not for a coward.

13. *Branwen's Cauldron (The Chessboard):*
restores the dead to life.

MORGAN LE FAY

Morgan Le Fay is the English name for the fairy who is best remembered from the tales of Arthurian legend. She has many names and there is confusion as to her exact parentage—which, being a fairy, stands to reason. The oldest records suggest she was the water nymph daughter of King Avallach, ruler of the sacred isle of Avalon. At his demise she took over as queen of the Enchanted Isle. Morgan was also known as Modron the river goddess or, sometimes, Matrona. In French, she is known as Morgaine La Fée and in Italian, Fata Morgana. Her other names include: Morgana the Lake Enchantress, Nimue (Merlin's love), and Viviane (Lady of the Lake and Lady of the Holy Isle). In Viviane's guise, Morgan was the fairy whose arm famously appeared from the water and took back Arthur's sword.

LEFT *Morgan Le Fay is known*
throughout the world for her
special fairy gifts.

The explanation for all these names is that Morgan is, in fact, all of these people. Her eight sisters were actually other emanations of herself, with the guise of Morgan Le Fay the ruling archetype.

Taught by Merlin, Morgan was a great healer fairy, and when she needed to travel swiftly, she would often turn into a bird. Because of her eight variations, the descriptions of Morgan differ. The most popular are as the water nymph Viviane, radiating an ethereal and otherworldly beauty of youth and purity, and as the strikingly beautiful and vivacious Queen of Avalon.

However, she is a fairy who can also be described simply by the colors of her sacred robes. As Morgan, her robes are opaline— that is to say, rainbowlike—reflecting the diversity of her character. When she takes on the appearance of the Triple Goddess occupied with her most sacred work, she wears the white robes of the Maid, the red robes of the Mother, or the black robes of the Crone. As the Lady of the Lake, her robes are blue and silver. In the role of a healer she appears in green and gold, and as the mystical priestess she wears purple. For fertility rites her robes are yellow, and for walking between worlds they are brown. Morgan Le Fay can never be pinned down to one appearance, but her overall magnificent beauty and magickal powers are legendary.

THE GREEN MAN

Immortalized by his magick symbol of a staff topped with a pine cone, the Green Man is one of the oldest images of the pagan Horned God—the pacifist, nature-loving god, Paganus, who ruled over fertility and the land. He is shown as brown or green in color and his face is made up entirely of oak leaves, fir and pine branches, and vines, reflecting the ancient belief that the head holds the essence of a spirit and immortality. The fir tree represents eternal time and the pine represents hope (in adversity). He wears adornments of acorns and berries between the many leaves and, because of the particular nature of fir and pine, his face reflects a timeless and wise appearance. He presides over the Eternal Forest and is also known as the Young Guardian of the Woodlands, Viridias. Images of the Green Man can be found carved in stone and wood throughout the world, and although some of the carvings have been altered over time to reflect the changing and fashionable views of spirituality, he is still one and the same, the father of all living creatures.

LEFT *A nature spirit of the oldest kind—the Green Man watches over our world.*

RIGHT *The face of the Green Man is made entirely of woodland leaves and berries.*

THE FISHER KING

Closely associated with the time of King Arthur, this legend can be found under different guises and in earlier times. The fairy version is this: the son of a sea god and a water nymph, the Fisher King was once a very wealthy fairy living in a grand castle, with lush meadows and fertile land all about him and throughout his kingdom. One day he was wounded in both thighs by an enemy fairy king with a magickal lance. His only hope of recovery was if the magickal Grail kept at his castle was used correctly by the Grail Hero, who was yet to come. While he waited for the Grail Hero, the Fisher King grew more

crippled, and his meadows and lands became barren and desolate. Soon his subjects were in poverty and the kingdom became a wasteland. The Fisher King took to fishing from the edge of a big lake, because that was now his only joy. While he waits, the lands remain barren, and if the Fisher King is not healed, neither will his lands recover.

Legend has it that one of Arthur's knights visited the Fisher King and saw the Grail. The Sea King and Water Nymph were also

BELOW *The King's wait may be symbolic of the longed for return of our own fairy world.*

present. The knight, whose name was Perceval (or Parsifal), noticed the Fisher King's terrible wounds but said nothing. He saw the Grail as well, but again was too polite to make comment. Because of this reticence, Perceval failed to heal the Fisher King or to acknowledge the Grail and ask a precise question of it. Since Perceval felt too humble to mention either the Fisher King's wounds or the beauty and purpose of the Grail, he clearly wasn't the Grail Hero after all. The following day, Perceval woke up to find the castle and the three fairies gone, and himself sitting upon a dry and dusty piece of land.

FAIRY QUEENS AND GODMOTHERS

Known as Titania (daughter of Titans) and Mab, the fairy High Queen of Great Britain is said to have her abode at Castle Chariot in Fairyland—it lies at Lyonness, somewhere between Land's End and the Isles of Scilly. However, many under-queens and their consorts rule the separate *sidhe* kingdoms of Britain and the rest of the world.

The fairy rade (or ride) is an important royal procession of fairies, led by their individual queens and kingly consorts. Mortal records report that those taking part are all exquisitely dressed and ride tiny white horses. The procession is full of magnificence and splendor, the queen with her consort, followed by the fairy knights and the aristocratic fairies, all passing through the human realms on a magickal pilgrimage.

LEFT *The very secret fairy rade is a blessing if seen by humans.*

The long manes and tails of the horses are braided with tiny flower heads, such as lily of the valley and forget-me-not, and thin white ribbons hung with softly tinkling gold and silver bells. The riders are even more gorgeously dressed in tiny, jeweled, colored velvets, silks, and satins, sewn with seed pearls and sparkling threads, each one wearing a miniature spiky crown crafted by the dwarves in priceless metals. The whole procession is bathed in moonshine and stardust, and the fairies that follow and run alongside sing out delicate and magickal songs, scattering gold dust and rose pollen.

It is a sign of good fortune to see a fairy rade go by and, whether you are observed by the fairies, or not, it is always wise to incline your head out of respect. And if you follow quietly for a while, you will undoubtedly see the whole procession disappear just before the entrance to an Otherworld place.

Fairy godmothers are tutelary fairies with the job of watching over human children. They are fairies that have reached a certain devotional level within the Otherworld, and are interested in positive connection with the human world, often as guardians to one particular family. Their particular magick emulates the magick of the Fates, and they can work wishes to benefit their chosen godchild. Protection, success, health, wealth, and beauty are the traditional magickal gifts for a fairy's godchild, usually given at the child's birth.

Due to the delicate and unusual nature of fairies, not every godmother is a good mother. Those who choose the malicious way are known as hags. Famous hags include Blue Cally of Ulster, who loses her powers when the spring comes, and Black Annis, a blue-faced hag from Leicestershire, in England.

WAR FAIRIES

The war fairies' main battle colors are blue or red, and white. Accompanied by fairy dogs, which are always white in color with red ears, war fairies have hair that is either naturally red or dyed red using a special decomposing moss. Their headdresses are adorned with bull-horns, a phallic symbol of fertility and protection; and raven wings, a symbol of the afterlife, or crane feathers, a symbol of sinister taboo. Their faces are adorned with magickal symbols painted in woad, and very little else in the way of clothing is worn. These are all specific adornments to give protection before going into battle. Carrying weapons made primarily of lead (the Otherworld metal used for effecting curses), they are renowned for sending the "fetch" (a person's ethereal double, or wraith) to their enemies just before their death or as an omen of their impending doom. War fairies, like war witches, dance clockwise inside stone circles before going

into battle, to gain the strength and protection of the Sun God; and counterclockwise for the protection and magick of the Moon Goddess. Famous war fairies, some of whom were also known as gods and goddesses in past times, include: Morrigan, the Raven War Goddess; Scathach, the Warrior Fairy Queen; Aífe, the Warrior Fairy Queen; and Andraste, the Goddess of Victory.

Marsh fairies, known as jack-o'-lanterns, were also a type of early war fairy, otherwise known as will-o'-the-wisps, or lantern men. They lived in swamps, seeking out enemy bands of warrior fairies and then leading them to treacherous marshes, where the fairy warriors would drown in the sinking mud. Each fairy band would whistle for their own lantern men and many horrible fairy deaths happened this way. Over time, as the fairy battles lessened and they were no longer needed, the lantern men would pick on any lonely human travelers they came across at night walking among the marshes. The rogue lantern men's lights and flames could be seen flickering in the distance and the exhausted traveler would follow the light gratefully, unaware of what lay before him. The only way to avoid the lantern men is to lie face-down in the marshes and wait until sunrise or until the ghostly lights have disappeared.

Border red caps are another type of war fairy, once thought to live on the borders of the Scottish Highlands and attracted to places with a violent history. These small fairies are called red caps because of their entirely red uniform and in particular their red caps, achieved by washing their clothes and hats in the blood of their slain victims. The red caps' mates are the Highland glaistigs, who appear in disguise to humans as

ABOVE *Carry a triage in a red kerchief if you feel there may be war fairies about.*

beautiful women. In reality, they are vampire fairies, who bite and suck the blood of anyone who dances with them. In order to protect yourself from this negative fairy, make a protective triage from a piece of lead, a twist of salt and a clove of garlic.

FAIRY FOOD

Oddly enough, it has been reported in some ancient texts that there are no dairy products in Fairyland, and as such these staples have to be "borrowed" from the human world. This would explain why supplies such as milk, cream, and butter sometimes seem to disappear from our homes more quickly than usual. And that is also why, if you disturb fairies in the cow shed or your kitchen, you may come across unexplained patches of milk, spilt as they skip hurriedly away with their spoils. Traditionally, fairy drinks and foods are made from the leaves of shrubs, flowers, and trees, sprinkled with magick and tasting of the most exotic flavors imaginable. Mushrooms are a great favorite of fairies, and they are connoisseurs of every variety. The exotic foods prepared for fairy parties can take on any sophisticated and exotic shape in order to lure the palates of human guests, but if you stray into Fairyland, you are warned never to eat or drink anything except water, because fairy food will bind you to that realm if you consume it. Red berries of the rowan tree are favorite fairy treats, although forbidden to humans. Ambrosia is made from the rare red wine belonging to the Greek Goddess Hera. When mixed with sacred herbs, it is said to confer immortality on those who drink it daily. Nectar is a delicious drink made from certain fairy beans and honey, and a glass can quieten the mind and give joy where there was sorrow. Never show greed in the presence of fairies: they truly dislike it.

FAIRY RINGS

Completely circular shapes growing in the ground, usually made up of mushrooms or daisies, are traditionally known as fairy rings. There is another different kind of fairy ring too, which is more subtle and shows grass growing out of kilter to the surrounding grasses and, in doing so, forming a circular pattern. This is where the fairies hold a party, usually around the time of the solstices, and dance around, wearing down the grass as they go into that most mystical of shapes, the circle. Fairies love dancing, so they plot out a circular ring boundary and then dance around and around until the crushed and flattened grass turns three times greener than the surrounding grass and shows a true fairy ring. Then the party begins within the ring. Fairy rings are not to be confused with crop circles, which are much larger and an altogether different kind of mystical experience. To see a fairy, try running around

ABOVE *Fairy rings are hard to find and must always be kept a secret.*

the outside of a fairy ring nine times in a counterclockwise direction and under the full moon. Also, if you stand inside a fairy ring under the full moon and make a wish, it is said that the wish will come true somehow. It is also believed that if you sit inside a fairy ring on Beltaine or Samhain (Halloween), not only will you see fairies, but there is every chance you may be taken away by them.

FAIRY FESTIVALS

The best times to look for fairies are at midnight or twilight when there is a full moon. Beltane, Midsummer, and Samhain are the three major pagan festivals that fairies celebrate. Cetshamain is a time for loud, raucous feasting and parties, where, due to its fertility emphasis, love magick is very popular. Midsummer is a fire-worshiping festival, where healing magick is rife, and Samhain is a time for more serious feasting and celebration, where, due to its emphasis on death and rebirth, communication magick is very popular. Another important festival is Lammas, where two rituals are always observed. The first is to make a "loaf mass," a wheaten bread offering to the Corn Goddess, which is made from the very first wheat gathered at harvest time. The second ritual is to make a "corn dolly," which is a figure of the Goddess made from woven stalks of wheat on the very last day of harvest, using the very last sheaves. This guarantees that the spirit of the Goddess dwells within the dolly and ensures a good harvest the following year.

SPECIAL DAYS

- *Lady Day (March 25): celebrating the power of women and their connection to the triple goddess (Lady Day is the older folk name for the Vernal Equinox.)*
- *Cetshamain (April 30– May 1): celebrating fertility rites and sexuality.*
- *Midsummer Solstice (June 21–22): celebrating the sun in its strongest and most magickal form.*
- *Lammas (August 2): celebrating the world's harvest.*
- *Samhain (October 31–November 1): celebrating the return of spirits from Summerland.*
- *Midwinter Solstice (December 22): celebrating the rebirth of the new Sun God and renewal of the land.*

FAIRY MUSIC AND LANGUAGE

Fairies adore music, dancing, fun, and laughter, and fairy music is the finest of all. Unfortunately, when overheard by humans, fairy music can bind them in a spell so that they cannot stop listening. It takes a great deal of control over the human mind to bring yourself out of a fairy trance.

Some fairies, such as fenshees (see page 70), excel in playing the fiddle specifically to enchant humans into an endless Otherworldly dance. In the main, they do it for their own entertainment, but if you cannot break free or they do not stop fiddling, it can have unhappy consequences. There are many ancient stories of humans being entranced in this way—so do take care if you hear the sweet strains of the fiddle wafting over the nighttime mists. Fairy magick should be worked with some vibration, music, or song for the best results. We cannot understand the language of fairies, but they can speak ours if they wish.

ABOVE *Listening to the fairies play may charm you more than you realize.*

FAIRY TIME AND TRAVEL

Midnight and twilight are the favored moments for fairy magick at the times of the full, new, or dark moon. There is a strange stillness in the air when fairies are about, and at twilight there is often an unusual amount of birdsong. Time passes on different levels and is endless in Fairyland, with fairies living until extreme old age and the physical signs of aging virtually unknown. Because of this, it is quite well known that people who have disappeared from this world for many years and then suddenly reappear are often under the impression that they went missing for only a couple of days. Time is quite different in Fairyland: for example, one year in Fairyland is said to be equivalent to around 365 years in the mortal world, but paradoxically one night in Fairyland is also said to be equal to ten years in this world. Stranger still, three days in a *si* (see page 12) can correspond to no time at all in this world. Which one is correct? All of them!

BELOW *Butterflies pull the leaf-chariots of little fairies who prefer to ride.*

Some people never come back from Fairyland: if you are intending to make a visit, it is wise to take a combination of useful and precautionary measures, such as wearing a garland of thyme and bay leaves around your neck to enable you to see fairies, wearing rowan twigs (mountain ash), verbain, and mistletoe in your hair for protection and to ensure a safe return to the mortal world, and carrying agate as an invisibility talisman.

Regarding travel, fairies fly in a variety of ways. Although most fairies have wings, a lot of the time these are purely decorative and not strong enough to lift them off the ground. The fairy broomstick is very small and made of a ragwort stem or pieces of straw. Merpeople like using boats or dolphins to cross the seas, whereas nixies prefer swans. Small earth fairies, such as dwarves and goblins, like to ride on ponies or goats. Even smaller fairies ride on butterflies, dragonflies, doves, peacocks, bats, and moths. If they don't use the travel services of a bird or animal, fairies can also wear tiny red caps that enchant them with a special flying power. Magickal words used by fairies and witches to lift them from the ground after preparing their rituals are; "Horse and hattock!", "Ho! Up and go!", "Thout, tout, throughout and about," or "Here's off, here's after."

FAIRY LORE

- Green is the color of the fairy world. Wearing green clothes aligns you to the fairies as a follower and ensures good luck.
- Fairy shrines should always face east so that as you pray and the fairies appear, you will catch the first glimpse of an enchanted moonrise.

- Glow worms provide fire for fairies to light their tapers, lanterns, and bonfires.
- Frogs and toads are used by fairies as messenger "mailmen," who deliver their tiny secrets without attracting attention.
- Birds are very special to fairies, being their equivalent to human cats or dogs. Dryads have the responsibility of teaching baby birds to sing and other fairies feed the fledglings with soft fruits and dead insects. If a bird's nest falls from a tree, fairies do everything they can to put it back.
- Wild white mice are used by aristocrat fairies to draw their opulent fairy carriages.
- Cobwebs, garlic, and honey are used by fairies for healing wounds. The cobweb is a bandage, the garlic an antiseptic, and the honey a soothing balm. Wrapped in thyme leaves, these make an excellent fairy offering. A similar offering kept in your home will ensure prosperity ahead.

LEFT *Birds and fairies often help each other and are very great friends.*

RIGHT *Sleeping fairies must
never be surprised, or bad
tempers may fly!*

- Fairy dust from an invisible hawthorn berry
is to be avoided at all costs—it is a potent
form of sleeping powder.
- An ancient recipe for an ointment to see
fairies is called the Magick Eye Ointment.
To make it, do the following: wash a glass
with rosewater and put it aside. Then, in a
mortar, put a tablespoon of walnut oil. Add
to this a pinch of salt, a handful of primrose
flowers, 3 hollyhock buds, 3 marigold buds,
3 hazel catkins, and a bunch of wild thyme.
Go to a fairy ring and pluck some grass
from within it and add this to the mixture.
Grind it all up and transfer the thick oil to
the rosewater glass. Leave this in sunlight
for 3 days. Then take a little of the oil and
smear it above your eyes on your forehead.
This should enable you to see fairies.
- Never disturb a sleeping fairy. They can
react so quickly that you may be harmed
even if the fairy is a good fairy.

- Fairy courtesans are very tiny fairies able to
fit into acorn cups or drown in dewdrops.
They serve as attendants to the Queen Fairy
and will enchant male humans, changing
them into tiny frogs for playmates.
- A huge cauldron, about one yard in
diameter, is kept in the thirteenth-century
village church of Frensham in England.
Legend has it that this cauldron was
borrowed from the fairies and never
returned. As a result, the fairies took the
magick from the cauldron and never lent
anything to the villagers again. Magickal
cauldrons and other objects are often
borrowed from the fairies and there are
many tales about them. If an object is not
returned, the fairies will dis-enchant it or

even break it, so the magick is destroyed. Fairies don't mind lending things, but you must always remember to give them back or risk some penalty.

• Never cut or harm a hawthorn tree, which is sacred to the fairies. If you must cut one down, you should always ask their permission. The hawthorn is the major plant used at the Cetshamain festival, where it is woven into circlets and worn in the fairies' hair. The hawthorn stands for hope and kisses, and by interweaving these two properties, the fairies send out a very obvious

LEFT *Fairy vegetation is full of secrets and magick that can benefit us all.*

message to prospective mates. Torches of burning hawthorn are also used to light the dance floors of the fairy glades. A hawthorn tree growing alone in a place, not surrounded by any other tree or plant, is called a fairy thorn, because it is a home special to the Fairy Queen of that place. A fairy thorn is also a sacred site, where you can leave offerings for the Fairy Queen in the hope that she will grant your wishes.

• Oak, ash, and thorn growing together are the three sacred trees of all fairies, known as the Sacred Tree Triad. It is said that, wherever these trees grow together there is a doorway to the Otherworld and a place where you may see fairies coming and going. The yew tree is also important to fairies because, as it can live for over a thousand years, it has become a symbol of everlasting life and is believed to protect the dead as they sleep.

- The foxglove plant (also known as folk's glove) is very popular with fairies, who wear the bells of the flower as hats or for the smaller fairies as dresses. The foxglove comes in many pretty colors and is a strong and durable petal, so it makes an ideal cloth for fairies.

- The whirlwinds of late summer at harvest time are known as the Winds of Change and the expression to "tip yer hat" is symbolically throwing a donation to the fairies into these magickal winds.

- To attract fairies, carry a four-leaf clover in your left pocket.

- Fairies are known to be extremely generous by nature. However, fairy gold can traditionally turn to dust in the human world, and fairy coins and jewels turn to rubbish after the fairy has left, especially if the fairy is cross with you for some reason. So, always leave some kind of gift, no matter how small, to thank the fairies, and you will be rewarded.

- Finally, a taboo that all fairies carry (with the sole exception of dwarves) is that they must never be touched by iron, because it has a burning effect on them. They can smell this mineral when it is carried, so never, ever carry iron in any form on your person when you're catching fairies. Perversely, iron is actually very good luck for mortals and is often used in fortune or protective spells. (In ancient times, humans believed it came to Earth as a gift from the gods in the form of a flaming meteorite, and called it "the metal from the sky.")

BAD FAIRIES

ABOVE *Bad fairies are thrown
out of Fairyland and delight
in upsetting others.*

Although in this book I have tried to present fairies in the best possible light, because of their naturally good and positive nature, it is true that sometimes fairies go bad. Examples include boggerts, brownies who have turned against humans but are not dangerous. Other fairies are simply made evil, like the yarthkins of Lincolnshire, England. The yarthkins were very small, ugly, and spiteful fairies, who delighted in hurting humans and doing evil. However, when the Lincolnshire Fens were eventually drained, the yarthkins disappeared too. The reasons for change from good to bad fairies are many and varied, rather like in human life, and if there are bad fairies about it is really the duty of their queen to deal with them. Most of the time, records show that bad fairies inevitably get what they deserve, but there are some fairies that slip through the net and live on the outskirts of mainstream Fairyland, seemingly delighting in making things go wrong. These fairies are different from naughty or mischievous fairies, because bad fairies really do mean trouble. By nature, fairies are easily offended and expect a

certain amount of kindness from humans before helping them out, so it is often the case that when a fairy has been insulted she will easily rise to the bait and give back ten times more anger than she felt. The story of Rumplestiltskin shows the typical behavior of a bad fairy, and the fairy Godmother in the story of Sleeping Beauty was by nature a very bad fairy. However, when she was slighted by not being invited to Aurora's christening, that particular fairy's rage and fury increased to overwhelmingly disproportionate levels of harm—something we might nowadays call "Fairy Rage."

Changelings are the result of bad fairy work. A changeling is a fairy baby that has been swapped with a human baby and left behind in the human baby's cot in the hope that the parents won't notice. Often reported as ugly or resembling grotesque old fairies, the changeling had a very hard time of it in

days gone by. In fact, if you suspect you have a changeling, the only thing to do is love it more than ever, because if you look after a changeling well, its true fairy mother will bless you and do everything she can to find the bad fairy that stole your child, and make them return it to you.

In modern times, there are still reports of new fairies and one of the most recent was the gremlin. Gremlins were apparently mischievous air sprites who had turned bad and made it their goal to interfere with airplanes, causing terrible results. The name was chosen by a British bomber squadron just before the outbreak of World War II and known about mostly by American and British pilots of that time. After that, gremlins stopped targeting only the air forces but seemed to turn up in any situation, hence the expression, "A gremlin in the works."

Nowadays, gremlins seem to be particularly fond of TVs and computers. This may be because of their increasing delight in any kind of negative energy—from simple bursts such as a bad news report or angry e-mail—to the Internet, a font of electrical energy, which along with positive vibes can hold a massive amount of negativity.

Fairies that cast curses are unhappy indeed, because they know that, despite the initial satisfaction they may feel, the curse will always rebound. Bad fairies inevitably attract a black-colored mist about them and in Fairyland it doesn't take long for other fairies to notice this. That is why bad fairies are often reported as living on their own, or in far-off places with difficult access. They are trying to keep away from the notice of their fairy queen and the justice that she will no doubt dispense.

BELOW *Light and love
are the best ingredients for
a fairy-filled home.*

The best way to protect yourself from the effects of a bad fairy is to always fill your house with airy and positive light. This counteracts the negative dark cloud that bad fairies attract, and cancels out the situation. If you are feeling particularly angry or hard done by, you must try to change that feeling into one of happiness and luck. If you stretch your mouth into a wide smile, no matter how bad you are feeling inside, if you can make your outer appearance smile, the inner smile will follow through. You might have to try this several times if you are feeling particularly swamped with negativity, but you will be surprised at the results. Change negative difficulties into positive successes, and you will never be bothered by a bad fairy. Ultimately, if you fill your days with music, light, and laughter, and your nights with sweet dreams and loving thoughts, you will be surely blessed from the Otherworld.

PART TWO

HOW TO CATCH FAIRIES

At this point, it is now up to you to decide whether you are interested in having a go at trying to catch a fairy yourself. With the knowledge of who they are and where they can be found, it is important to understand how to commune with fairies. This means in the first instance to become aware of them, as well as seeing and talking to them (which usually happens later). Although some people can "hone in" on fairies immediately, the almost trancelike mental state that you need to acquire is extremely important if you expect to communicate with fairies. Suppose that you have read one of the chapters and chosen a fairy whom you would like to meet. Having completed the relevant ritual, you may be back at home wondering why they

ABOVE *Catching fairies*
should enrich and enchant
your life forever.

are not standing in front of you. Well, it
doesn't always happen like that. Some fairies,
like nymphs, prefer to stay in their indigenous
homes, no matter how hard you try and catch
them. For fairies that prefer not to follow, you
have to make special visits to them, perhaps
at their shrines, but that is like visiting a very
special friend and so is perfectly fine.

If, when you are at home, you wonder
whether there are any invisible fairies about
you, there is a simple meditational spell that
you might like to do (see page 47), which
should relax your outer awareness and help
you concentrate on your inner sixth sense. It
is when we are in this state that we can hear
and see fairies with no problem at all. The
first thing you need to get to grips with is the
automatic response of most people when
faced with the possibility of meeting fairies,
which is disbelief, suspicion, and/or doubt. By
nature, we are wary of being taken for fools:

that is part of our survival mechanism, after
all. However, at some point, if we really do
want to travel in the mystic realms, we have
to turn our backs on those pre-programmed
defenses and give ourselves the possibility
of opening up to another level. You cannot
enter the mystic world with feelings of doubt
or suspicion, because these are negative
influences that hinder your progress. If we
tried, I am sure we could all find reasons not

survival mechanism, we can all doubt proof if we want to, no matter how well presented it might be. The fact of the matter is that proof doesn't really come into it—it's truth you need, and the only way to experience the truth is to see it for yourself. So scientific minds, sadly, are missing out enormously on a whole other quantum experience. Here is what I suggest, instead:

to do anything at all, but in order to move forward we have to overcome our reservations and take a chance. There may be occasions when you feel like a fool or doubt the effectiveness of a certain ritual, but like any learning process, these are just small weeds in a blooming garden. If you can pull out these "weeds" or walk over them, you will eventually get to the beautiful garden beyond. If a person tells me he needs "scientific proof" before venturing further, I feel very sorry, because, to my mind, that person has missed the point altogether. The proof comes from finding it yourself; no one can prove it to you. Again, because of our

---

BE OPEN

i   Discard your need for "proof"

ii   Open your mind to any possibility

iii   Let yourself encounter "weeds" on your search

iv   Accept those results that you can't explain

v   Know that you are protected at all times

vi   Believe that all things are possible

MIND CONTROL

Having taken this list as a starting point, now light some sandalwood incense and lie down on a bed, sofa, or carpet and begin to relax until you are comfortable (you may like a pillow under your head). A chant that I use and which is very effective are the words, "Nyam, yo ho, renge, ko." If you repeat these words over and over, you will see that they fall into a lilting rhythm and, then, as you get more relaxed, the words join together almost into one musical tone. You should attempt to get to this stage before going further. It is very fulfilling to achieve this state and easy to continue chanting for hours, although this is not the intended goal. This chanting connects you to an astral force, and achieving that link successfully will ensure that it is always open to you.

Having chanted for perhaps a half-hour, let the notes fade away. Close your eyes and let any image fall before you. You may think you can see only a "darkness" but if you accept that this "darkness" is the canvas, you should soon be able to see outlines within the darkness. The more you relax, the more your sixth sense will take over and detailed images should fill your mind. There is no point in "straining your eyes" to see something; visualization is not like seeing with the eyes. You have to try and let the images come to you. In a sense, you are seeing with your "third eye" and, similar to a night vision camera, the images will be strange and unusual to you at first.

When you have reached this stage, it is possible that, through the power of visualization techniques, you could progress in a different direction to one of the many other branches of mystical work, such as remote viewing, astral scrying, self-healing, and so forth. However, If you are attempting to commune with fairies, it is best to remain relaxed but bring yourself back to awareness of your physical surroundings.

Open your eyes and let the images flood into you, rather than particularly focusing on

BELOW *A fairy may appear when you least expect it to!*

what you can see. It is at this point that many people see things flashing past the corner of their eyes and so forth, and this is usually the first appearance of a fairy.

With this new way of looking at things, carry on with your normal life, because you will have opened a part of you, deep within, that will now let you see fairies when they are around. If you accept fairies, they will accept you. The first time I saw Tigire (see page 83), his face was so defined in the surroundings of my bathroom wall that I was almost shocked into looking away. When I looked back, the face I had seen had reverted to a pattern in the molding wallpaper. I chose at that moment to accept that Tigire was there and so I looked a third time, with these new eyes, and the sharp definition of his face was back again. The more I looked, the more he appeared. Later, having cleaned the moldy wall, Tigire's face could still be seen peeping out at me. Then, while out and about, I started seeing the same face on brick walls or in café gardens and I accepted once again, with new eyes, that Tigire was following me about. The more I got into this, the more I could see. When his name popped into my head on demand, I knew for sure that I had attracted a little fairy to me. While skeptics would no doubt have a ready explanation that I am imagining these things, my answer would be that this imagination is reality and it is they who are missing it.

It is the childlike belief that we all lose so quickly in life that is the key to unlocking the Otherworld, and if we can find that innocent belief, once more, we will discover the keys to everything else that we are looking for in our lives.

RIGHT *Fairy faces may be seen in all manner of natural objects.*

COMMUNICATING
WITH FAIRIES

Two excellent ways of communicating with invisible fairies are by earth divination and secret symbols.

Earth divination can take many forms, from reading melted candlewax images in a bowl of water to throwing a scoop of soil onto the ground and reading the patterns that it makes. Before attempting any form of geomancy, however, it is important to magnetize (using prayer or chants) the materials that will be used to throw or drip, and consecrate (using salt or holy water) the ground or bowl that the seer uses for a base.

Secret symbols are connected to natural objects: for example the Beth-Luis-Nion (the secret tree alphabet that holds the symbols to all of nature's secrets) or simpler forms such as twigs or leaves left on the ground, on stones or tree stumps. In the simpler form, a few of the main symbols used are: X, which means "no good"; double X, which means "a fight"; the diamond, which means "successful times"; and the bars TTT, which mean "danger." Two horizontal sticks mean "not welcome here." A horizontal stick with a cross above means "you are welcome to stop here." This is a nature-based form of communication that is constantly changing.

With these examples in mind, think of other symbols you could make with sticks and leaves. The more you practice, the more your mind will accept this unusual language and the easier it will become to read.

If you want to ask a fairy a question, leave a message on a stone or on the ground in your garden and then come back the next day and see if it has been rearranged or removed. Alternatively, try to increase your fortune by making these symbols and keeping them about your home.

SECRET SYMBOLS

The Diamond. This means "Good Fortune and Success."

The X shape. This means "No Good."

Two Horizontals. This sign means "Not Welcome."

The Double X. This means "A Fight is Coming."

Three T-shapes. This sign means "Danger Here."

The X and Vertical. This sign means "Change Direction."

BANSHEE

RIGHT *After hearing a banshee's cry, you must let her go to continue her work.*

The majority of *bean sidhe* (see page 12) are those better known as banshee, the famous and rather macabre fairies that wail, scream, and lament at the time of someone's death. In fact, the banshee is actually providing a service, because once the household has heard the cry of the banshee it is more able to accept the situation or, in some cases, get prepared for an all-out fight for survival! The banshee looks very pale and thin, with long white or gold hair and dark blue eyes. She is a very beautiful-looking fairy and a death messenger. When someone is close to death, she will come to the window and let out a certain amount of shrieks, corresponding to the amount of days that person has left to live— for example, if she shrieks three times, that person has three days, and so on. If a banshee shrieks once, the passing over is imminent. She is not really a fairy that you

TO CATCH A BANSHEE

Take a glass bottle with a stopper and put in it 5 drops of spring water, a small amount of myrrh oil, and a teaspoon of baking soda wrapped in a twist of silver paper. Leave the bottle on its side under a bush and hold on to the stopper. All fairies have a certain amount of curiosity and the banshee should get close to the bottle (attracted to the Underworld scent of baking soda and myrrh and to the shine of the silver) and then she may try and get into the bottle, dissolving like a wisp of cloud. At this point you must rush to put the stopper into the bottle and then you will have her. You must be quick, however, because the minute a banshee knows she has been tricked, she will be out of that bottle in a nanosecond.

should catch since her job is death messenger, and if you keep her in your house, she cannot alert others. Also, she will probably keep you awake all night with her screaming. If, for some reason, you had to catch a banshee (and I really don't recommend you try), the justification would have to be something like when you fear for the health of another and would like confirmation of their prospects of survival.

BROWNIE

RIGHT *Brownies like nothing better than keeping a house clean, neat, and tidy*

Also known as house brownies because of their love of housework, these little fairies are the best of companions. However, they do have a naughty streak, particularly when they feel wronged. Brownies often dance in saucers of milk and food left out for your cat or dog, and the way to tell if a brownie has been there is to look at the patterns their tiny feet have made around the saucers. Inquisitive by nature, brownies are the fairies that take little objects from around the house to examine and sometimes use. Needles, pins, anything small and shiny, brownies will take quite happily and hide from you, unless you specifically ask for them back. Light and dark brown and sometimes purple in color, with pale blue eyes and thick, shaggy, brown hair, brownies are small (around 3 feet high) with delicate features and large pointed ears. Their wings are small and brushlike, and they are

TO CATCH A BROWNIE

Old houses often have brownies living there already, especially if the house seems naturally clean, neat, and tidy. However, if you can't detect the presence of a brownie, here is a very ancient instruction for catching one. Find three hazel sticks. Strip back the bark on each and write your name on one stick, the brownie's name on the second, and draw a five-pointed star on the third. Bury the sticks at the edge of a graveyard, preferably under a yew tree, and leave them there for exactly one week. Then dig up the sticks, take them home, and keep them somewhere safe. Call for the brownie whenever you like and you should get an almost instant result. Leave the brownie alone and you will gradually gain a caring friend.

often seen carrying things in their arms as they hop and flit about your home. Brownies don't usually bother with clothes as a rule; the most they might wear is a small collection of rags, but usually nothing at all. It is well known that if you give a gift of smart clothing to brownies, they will leave you immediately. It is not entirely certain whether this is because they are insulted by the gift and disappear to be by themselves in their raggedy altogether, or whether they are happy to finally have a smart suit!

DRYAD AND HAMADRYAD

Every tree, bush, or thicket growing has a female dryad and hamadryad spirit joined to it. Able to separate from its wooden host, the dryad is a type of nymph (see page 102). They are the ancient guardians of trees, much communicated with and contacted by Druids for inspiration and advice. Hamadryads, however, are the life spirits of the tree, who are born when the tree grows and die when the tree dies. They are protected by the dryad. It is important that you always commune first with the dryad and hamadryad spirit of a tree before taking away any part of it—wood, bark, leaves, berries, or flowers. This will enable the tree spirit to prepare itself and enhance magickal properties into the removed part for your use. After removing any part of the tree, you should always leave an offering as an exchange and token of thanks.

TO CATCH A DRYAD/HAMADRYAD

Grow a tree in your garden or in a special and secret place. Once the tree takes root and lives, the spirit of the tree, the hamadryad, comes alive. Get to know the personality and appearance of your hamadryad by visiting the tree regularly, talking with its spirit, and leaving gifts. Hugging a tree is, in fact, to hug a hamadryad, and the energy and peace that you can obtain by doing this very simple act is worth any self-consciousness that you might initially feel. When the tree decays or dies, then the hamadryad will pass over to the Otherworld while the wooden remains return to the comfort and peace of the Earth. Love your hamadryad, and your hamadryad will love you.

RIGHT *You can see a dryad most clearly if you look from the corner of your eye.*

WARF

RIGHT *Dwarfs traditionally find goats very comfortable to ride on!*

Male dwarfs are very small, dark-skinned people, much mentioned in Norse mythology, and vary in size from 2 inches to 2 feet in height. They are traditionally of wizened face and hunched back, with large heads and long beards. They live to a ripe old age and their feet are often shaped like goat's hoofs (although they don't have goat's legs). They choose to ride goats as their main source of transportation instead of the usual dragonflies, butterflies, and birds favored by most other small fairies. Their jobs are centered around magick metalworking, using primarily gold, silver, bronze, and copper, and there are many famous stories about their wonderful work, particularly with reference to magickal tools, armor, and protective talismanic and amuletic jewellery. They have the gift of invisibility, can appear and disappear instantaneously, and are difficult to catch.

TO CATCH A DWARF

Go to a wooded area and dig a small hole in the ground. On a piece of black paper, write your name in gold ink and then underneath that, write down the particular problem you are experiencing or need help with. Fold and leave the paper within the hole, then place a red apple on top. Fill in the hole, making it look as undisturbed as possible. Now go home and look out for your fairy guest or a result to your problem. You will know instantly when the magick starts.

Apples are underworld fruits full of magick and power.

They are also very good at changing shape when in a tight spot. Dwarf males usually wear black, brown, or gray clothes so that they can merge with their surroundings. The females prefer white, gold, and silver clothes, reflecting their joy of light and the sun. The males live mainly in dark and secret places, such as mountains and caves, and always in tribal groups. Each group is ruled over by a King Dwarf and a tribal chieftain, who controls the vast armies of war dwarfs. The King Dwarf rules over the tribe and the tribal

chieftain is concerned with war, righting wrongs, and guarding the huge underground caves of precious metal and stones that the dwarfs traditionally work with. Strangely enough, the dominant sex of the dwarf race is male, but when you hear about the females they are invariably described in terms that sound as if they belong to a different species. Most dwarf females are taller, around 3 inches to 3 feet, extraordinarily beautiful, fair-haired and fair-skinned, in direct contrast to their darker masculine counterparts. They are also much younger-looking in appearance. The other difference between male and female dwarfs is that the male of the species turns to stone when in direct sunlight, which means he can come out safely only at nighttime, whereas, paradoxically, the female thrives in the sun and is often spotted during the daylight hours. I suppose this would explain why there are more male dwarfs living in dark and damp caves than females. Another interesting fact about dwarfs is that they are famous for being extremely wise and holders of secret knowledge. They are very adept at looking into the future and are known to be particularly concerned about the way mortals live in modern times, with regard to the food that humans consume and the pollution they generate. According to dwarfs, eating bad food is the reason why humans die so early. However, to humans they are fond of or adopt, the dwarf will be a constant source of wise information and support, and is therefore a guest to be treasured. Passing on secret magickal information in words, runes, and song, dwarfs are a bonus to any household, but they must like you to be of any use, otherwise you may find you've got more than you bargained for. If you treat a dwarf with respect and love, he will return your kindness and may reward you with priceless gifts.

L F

RIGHT *Elves will always reward kindness with good fortune.*

Elves are small, mischievous fairies, green in color, who love hunting, riding, and shooting at humans. The cattle that elves are responsible for are deer. Their favorite colors are brown, red, and green. Elves traditionally grow to a maximum height of 3 feet and are small, enchanted beings with small, fat noses tilting up at the ends; thick, usually red hair; and sharp, brown eyes. Elves are also known as pixies, piskies, and sprites. They are divided into two variants; dark and light. The dark elves prefer to live below ground, in places such as underground caves, deep within hill mounds, and barrows, drains, and cellars. They keep to themselves and come out willingly only at nighttime. Light elves on the other hand, prefer to live above ground, in places such as forests, woods, ruins of castles, and abandoned houses, and are quite fond of mortals. They are all of them famous

TO CATCH AN ELF

Make or buy an elf horn or tiny wooden instrument, such as a pipe. Take it to an elven site, such as a hill, wood, or ruined place. Blow the horn three times, shouting, "Elven, elven, elven, gracious thanks, come to me." Now turn once counterclockwise. Blow the horn three times more, shouting, "Elven, elven, elven, I have need of thee." Now turn counterclockwise twice. Blow the horn again three times more, shouting, "Elven, elven, elven, it is done so mote it be." Now turn counterclockwise three times and say, "Blessed be." Finally, snap the little instrument in two pieces and leave one at the site and take the other piece home with you. Your elf friend should follow soon after.

for their somewhat dry sense of humor. Light elves are working fairies, who help both inside and outside the home with any hard work that mortals might have. Modern elves are particularly fond of garages and are famous for finishing off jobs that have been forgotten or delayed. They usually do this when you leave something for over a week or go away for a while. Dark elves, on the other hand, prefer to remain underground and dream up ways of teasing humans while they forge their tiny and annoying weapons.

Elves get bored if left alone for too long with no one to talk to: opposite are some of their naughtier pastimes.

There is a place named Pudding Pie Hill, supposedly located in Yorkshire, England. It is known to be the chief home of the dark elves, an enchanted hill brought to life by those who live deep within it, and is said to be a good place to find an elf.

Both types of elves are particularly good at sensing human emotions. If they think you fear or are nervous of them, they will be more likely to play tricks on you. They also take exception to very strong smells such as aftershave! To please an elf or to try and get on its good side, you could leave out a gift such as an egg, which is symbolic to all fairies that they will never go hungry at your house, or you could try plaiting 3 red strands of wool and hanging an elf-shot flint from the door of your house to warn them off.

Elf locks Knots that appear in your hair or your animals' hair overnight, where the elves have been playing while you slept. The way to protect yourself from elf locks is to decorate a birch twig with red, black, and white ribbons and put it under your pillow or next to the animals' sleeping quarters.

Elf arrows Made by dark elves, these are the miniature flint weapons often found scattered around fields and woods. If you've been harmed by an elf arrow, the remedy is said to be to bathe in water that has had an elf arrow and piece of lemon soaked in it overnight.

Elf shot Again, the responsibility of the dark elves, these fairy darts have poisonous tips and are sold to other fairies as weapons for spreading diseases. They are much smaller in size than elf arrows. If you have been elf-shot, check for any illness and go seek medical advice. However, if there are no visible signs of disease but you still feel you may have been

elf-shot, a bath in warm water with a tablespoon of natural salt crystals is said to be just the thing to put yourself right.

Elf-marked If you have strange or particular birth marks on the face and/or body, these are usually said to be a sign of the elven world and may signal your elven ancestry.

Elf horns Tiny wooden or bone instruments, which elves use to call each other and play music.

FAIRSHEE (FAIR SIDHE)

Fairshees are one of the little fairy men of the hill and are also incredibly beautiful to look at—so much so that it is virtually impossible not to fall in love once you have been visited by a fairshee. The fairshees are male fairies that visit you mostly when you are sleeping. They can be any shape, size, or color, but in their natural form revert back to small stature (around 5 feet) and fine features. They are full of love and desire for human females and it can be great fun to spend time with them. As well as this, fairshees often visit in dreams to give you advice when you are in trouble. However, he will always break your heart because the fairshees belong to no one, and once you have fallen in love with a fairshee, he will most surely move on, and you must take care not to pine listlessly for evermore without him. Fairshees are possibly the fairies most women want to catch, and they are

probably the hardest to do so because they are a complete paradox. The only way you would ever catch a fairshee is by not appearing to want to catch him at all (and when you are under his spell, that may be the most difficult thing to try and remember). A friend of mine once fell deeply in love with a fairshee and for a while it was wonderful, but as the intensity of her emotions grew, the fairshee's visits became less and less frequent until he came no more. Eventually, with our help, she did manage to get on with her life and involve herself with humans again, and strangely enough, the fairshee came back, albeit temporarily. This time, she knew not to try and hold on to him, and as a result of this new knowledge, the fairshee visits her more and more often, as he will. She has come to accept his surprise nocturnal visits when they happen and is full of love for his company,

but when he goes, she has finally accepted that he will go and does not expect him to stay. He knows she has acquired this knowledge, and seemingly as a result, he stays longer—hence the paradox.

A fairshee carries in his pockets that most enviable potion; the Fairy Sleeping Dust. This is made from an invisible hawthorn berry that can be seen only in its natural habitat when

TO CATCH A FAIRSHEE

To catch a fairshee, you must first ignore him. A fairshee will turn up in your dreams when you least expect it. For example, if you have been thinking about fairshees for a week or so, and nothing has happened, it is almost entirely certain that the minute you stop trying to dream of him, he will undoubtedly visit you.

Here's a special tip regarding fairshees: you should wear a thin garland of thyme around your neck before sleeping in order to see him. If you want to attract a fairshee, hold a small bunch of straw in your right hand before going to sleep, and if you want to send him on his way, then hold a small bunch of vervain in your right hand. You can be absolutely sure that he will know the meaning of these secret fairy messages. Once you have dreamed of your fairshee, you can then try and hold onto his image during the day. Consciously remember everything about your dream, bringing it alive as you go about your day, and then, before sleeping, know in your heart that you will see him again. As you get used to doing this, the fairshee will be attracted to you more and more and should become a regular visitor in your dreams. Never get heavy with a fairshee and then he will stay around forever!

LEFT *Thyme is a famously magickal herb used for its power of attraction.*

viewed facing the east at moonrise. This potion is very sacred and if you are ever lucky enough to meet and talk with a fairshee, it will be because he has undoubtedly sprinkled you with some! Surrounded by delicate lights, the fairshee is guided in his nocturnal wanderings by little fleets of glow worms, who provide him with fairy fire to light his footsteps. As one of the aristocratic band of fairies, the fairshee has an opulent and extravagant nature. Do not be surprised at anything you might experience while in his company—even if you are reduced in size and whisked off in a golden carriage drawn by wild white mice!

Fairshees traditionally visit at nighttime and there are certain ways in which you can attract them. First, your bed should be facing from the east (head) towards the west (feet), so he will see you immediately when the sun sets at night. Second, never "air" or turn over

RIGHT *Holding the vervain herb will clearly tell your fairshee to go away.*

your mattress on a Friday, Saturday, or Sunday. These are his favorite days to visit, but if the bed has been turned, this will create an "empty" image, as if you weren't there, and the fairshee will turn away.

F ENSHEE (FEN SIDHE)

Fenshees are another type of fairshee, who live in vast tracts of boggy marshland. They are particularly good at playing music, and their favorite instruments are the reed pipes and drums. They hide from people in the foggy mists that invariably surround marshland, and if you get lost and hear the pipes or drums playing, be very careful about following the music. People have been known to wander for days, lost in the mists and marshes, with only the beguiling sound of pipes and drums to encourage them further. Fenshees are again mostly small of stature (around 4–5 feet) and fine featured, but have a more wild look about them. Their long, wiry hair tends to vary in color, from white through varying degrees of blond and yellow to light brown, often worn in a ponytail, and they nearly always sport a mustache, or beard, or both. Their favorite garb seems to be tight-

TO CATCH A FENSHEE

Take a friend with you for this one, as the ritual can take all night and you don't want to be alone for all that time while you are casting spells. Go to the edge of a marshland and make your own fairy ring of 13 white stones and sit inside it with a musical instrument of some sort in front of you. Light a silver candle and softly and gently play the instrument. If a fenshee appears, move the stone nearest to him to offer a doorway into the fairy ring. Never once look the fenshee in the eye, or he will be startled and frightened off. Keep playing your music until dawn, when the fenshee will be caught inside your instrument and bring you acclaim as a musician, a poet, or a singer.

fitting, straight-legged trousers, flowing shirts, and waistcoats, and they often wear red scarves or kerchiefs around their necks. Fenshees have very bony and transparent wings, which reach to the ground when folded and rise high above their heads when fully opened. Various instruments hang around their bodies such as pipes on strings, lutelike guitars on their backs, cymbals, triangles, drums, and so forth.

IREFAY

RIGHT *Portunes and firefays are thought to make their homes inside pieces of straw.*

The firefays are tiny little brothers to salamanders and are often confused with wiskies (see page 126), although firefays are red in color and wiskies are smaller and black. Firefays are also sometimes confused with the very ancient fairies called portunes. (About $\frac{1}{8}$ inch high, portunes look like miniaturized and extremely elderly humans.) Firefays are humanlike in appearance with long, narrow, transparent wings and are also about $\frac{1}{8}$ inch tall. They are usually found outside, hanging around bonfires, volcanoes, and hot bubbling springs. It is very rare to find a firefay on its own—they live in groups of hundreds and do everything together. Their sustenance is taken from the fumes given off by fires and hot places, and they can be seen in groups hovering just above the flames, dancing and singing madly when they are feeding on the fire's metaphysical effluence.

TO CATCH A FIREFAY

The very best time to catch a firefay is sometime between Samhain (October 31) and up to and including the fire festival on November 5. Light a bonfire safely and throw on to it equal amounts of dried primrose, dried bay leaves, and dried bog myrtle leaves. As the herbs spit and crackle, draw a metal strainer quickly over the top of the bonfire and place it, open-end down, on the earth. Your firefays will be caught within it and you can now make three wishes while you hold them. Then turn up the strainer to let them go, and they will fly off and endeavor to make your wishes come true.

FLOWERFAY

RIGHT *Beautiful flowerfays can be found in every flower-growing garden.*

Very delicate fairies, these are the spirits of the flowers themselves, emulating almost exactly the colors and appearance of the flowers they come from. Distant cousins to dryads, flowerfays are very tiny and ethereal, with large delicate and beautifully colored wings that are unusually strong. They speak in an unknown language and can be seen shivering excitedly when emotionally charged. They travel on the backs of dragonflies and butterflies, but only within a short distance of their flower homes. Flowerfays bring lightness into your life and are particularly good for anyone recuperating from any kind of illness. Always treat them with great care and sensitivity—carry on as normal if ever you glimpse one and never subject them to loud noises. Remember to keep this advice in mind, and you are likely to be rewarded when you ask for a wish.

TO CATCH A FLOWERFAY

First choose the kind of flowerfay you would like in your home. Then either dig up the plant from your garden, or buy one from a garden center. Put it in a pot with plenty of room and water it regularly, keeping it out of direct sunlight. Place a plaited wreath of the herb rue around the rim of the flowerpot. Talk regularly to the flower and as it grows and blooms, you should start to notice a different feeling around the pot, as if someone may be watching you. The more you look after your flower, the more the fairy will become visible to you. Leave small, unexpected gifts for the fay from time to time within the circlet of rue, and if you need a favor or wish, ask the flower directly.

_G_ IANT

Giants were an ancient race of gigantic half-fairy, half-human beings, who have seemingly disappeared from the world and into the relative safety of folklore for a very good reason. Mentioned in the Bible and elsewhere as sons of Heaven and close to God (despite their frightening stature and appearance), giants were originally described as tall, strong, and beautiful, and were believed to be the personification of the natural universe in human form. Kindly creatures but with a propensity to slow-wittedness, giants enjoyed games of strength and suchlike, which tested their skills and pitted their immense physical abilities against each other. To this day you can still see large stone blocks and bolders that are randomly strewn across the Earth where the giants left them. The ancient Egyptians, Greeks, and Romans all left behind depictions of giants in huge sculptures and monuments. For example, the Colossus of Rhodes and the fantastic statues depicting the Pharoahs were built to reflect the importance of the giant spirit within their own people. Legend has it that the Roman emperor Maximus was very large (around 9 feet tall), which may have reflected his descent from the giant race. The story of giants is a sad one, because being neither totally human nor totally fairy, giants were rejected by both races. Ridiculed by fairies and attacked by humans, they were forced to fight back, and through this change of character became feared as bad-tempered monsters. Eventually, most of the giant race chose to die out and take ghostly occupation of large, natural objects such as volcanoes, mountains, and vast lakes, where they could be left in peace. Nowadays, surviving giants may be smaller in size and similar to humans. However, they

have kept their original heroic abilities as a
form of magick deep within their spirits. To
look at, they may appear to be no different
from any other human, but their actions and
deeds will always speak volumes. If you are
able to catch a giant's spirit within you, it will
enlarge your life experiences and open up a
new way of thinking which will bless you
in return.

TO CATCH A GIANT

The essence of a giant is found in his noble spirit. In these days, the noble giant spirit can be found only where it rests, inside mountains and other large natural domains. In order to catch a giant, it is necessary to know that you will be catching his essence and keeping it within you, hopefully incorporating that gentle wisdom in all you do from then on. Firstly, you have to make a special divining item that will confirm whether you are near giants. Take a loaf of bread and cut it in half. Take a white candle, and scoop out a tiny bit of the bread from the middle and place your candle inside the hole, so that the bread becomes a candle holder and can sit alone with the candle upright in its center. The candle represents fire, which represents the soul. The bread represents the host, which represents the body. Now visit a large, natural domain, such as a mountain or volcano. Place your candle in its holder at the foot of the mountain and light it. If the flame is extinguished by any natural force, then there is no giant within that mountain. If the flame burns steadily, you are on the right track. Walk around the candle nine times, clockwise, in the direction of the sun and chant, "Giant within, come in," over and over, until you have finished walking. Now place your hands on the ground and mentally invite the giant that lives within the mountain to occupy your life in safety and goodness. When you are ready, extinguish the candle while visualizing the giant's spirit leaving his stone-filled home and entering the warmth and safety of your life. Now you carry his qualities with you.

RIGHT *A candle is the guiding light which attracts a giant's soul.*

All fairies are very fond of pigs, but giants particularly so. Pigs like music and are extremely intelligent—they also have the same inherent kindness as giants and like being made a fuss of and paid attention to.

Pigs are also able to "hear" the wind mystically. When storms are gathering, a pig will usually inform you by becoming restless or squealing. Never deliberately harm or starve a pig, or you will upset a giant.

G NOME

RIGHT *Gnomes make great
cleaners, but prefer to keep
to themselves.*

Elemental spirits of the Earth, gnomes are close relatives to dwarfs and leprechauns, and distant relatives to trolls and hobgoblins. They guard the treasures of the Earth. Both male and female, gnomes are kind little people, with strange white eyes that have a vertical black pupil. The eyes are usually the first thing you notice about gnomes: they shine out at you from the depths of their homely faces and curtain of thick, dusty, and tangled hair. Preferring to live underground, they are usually around 1½ inches tall, but when confronted by danger can stretch to the largest size imaginable. They are quite shy and do not like human company. Unlike their dwarf cousins, however, they will be the most faithful of servants once caught. But you must treat them well, because they have a malevolent streak that will become apparent when the gnome feels it has been wronged. Gnomes have no problem with hierarchy or social structure. They treat everyone in the same way, which is to say, calmly and fairly. Gnomes also have a particular horror of loud noises (but not loud music), and their laid-back attitude creates calm and peace wherever they are found. However, the ringing of church bells and noise of machinery can upset them very much. Both sexes mostly favor wearing green-colored clothes and are particularly fond of little red hats with bright yellow or white feathers in them. They also like big, lace-up, hob-nailed boots, and the female gnome wears hundreds of petticoats, trailing gray, dusty, and torn lace behind her. Not hugely bothered by personal hygiene, they are completely happy to clean up other people's houses, and make an excellent addition to any home.

TO CATCH A GNOME

My own group of gnomes just appeared one day in the wall of my bathroom. The leader is called Tigire, and although he comes and goes at will, he always appears if I specifically call him. When I first saw Tigire, I was a little alarmed by how fierce he looked. His eyes were white with very black, slitted pupils, but as soon as I got to know him and after he had told me his name (I asked him aloud and the answer immediately popped into my head), I began to see what a dear and clever friend I had been lucky enough to make. (Mind you, it took about a week of talking before he felt happy enough to listen to me.) Tigire then brought a group of other small fairies to visit and they could often be found flitting about the walls of my bathroom, sometimes teasing each other and playing leapfrog. Perhaps you might like to call to my friend Tigire, and see if he will visit your bathroom, too. Otherwise,

I would suggest looking very carefully around any damp areas in your house, particularly if you happen to have mold growing anywhere. Gnomes often use patterns in mold to communicate with mortals. If you see the outline of a gnomish face or body, look carefully and often at the pattern. It should become clearer as the gnome materializes, until one day it may wink at you or even jump out and stand before you. Failing that, you could create your own mold by growing it in a jar with some bread and water and see what comes with it. Most fairies are allergic to iron because it burns them. However, underground fairies such as gnomes and dwarves often come across and work with this metal and have built up an immunity to its powerful properties. So, as iron is a good-luck metal for humans, you can safely use this as part of your attraction spell to catch a gnome.

GWYLLION

RIGHT *Gwyllions are clever with money and will help you if they decide to stay.*

Fierce mining mountain fairies about 18–20 inches high, these are usually found in Wales, where they can be heard knocking on the cave walls where rich mineral deposits are found. Both light- and dark-skinned, with jet black hair and a penchant for gold teeth and earrings, they are particularly fond of wearing brightly colored, striped clothing most of the time, and keep plain white outfits for special occasions. If you hear the knocking or singing of a gwyllion while mining, you can be certain that where the noise is, so too is a rich vein of ore, and if you are quick enough to break through the rock, you may just catch them at their work. Gwyllions use very tiny miniature tools in their work, which are affected by very special magick. I myself have a tiny gold hammer and saw, which I believe once belonged to a gwyllion, and that I treasure and use in my personal geomancy.

TO CATCH A GWYLLION

Miners traditionally leave a didjan (small piece) of dinner in their places of work specifically for the gwyllion to find and eat. Go to the place where you have heard the gwyllion singing and working, leave out a small cloth with some food and drink on it, and then sit to one side and wait. A gwyllion will come with you only if it wants to, so there is no need to try and catch it. However, always treat a gwyllion with respect—these hardworking little fairies have surprisingly large tempers when upset. When you see the gwyllion or feel its presence, wrap up the remains of the victuals in the cloth and leave it buried there. Return home and talk out loud to the gwyllion, who will hear you.

If you are looking for gwyllions in caves or the Welsh countryside, you can leave a sign for those fairies that you are a friendly human. Simply pour a jug of beer in a circle shape around the place that you are looking and then come back the next day to see if there has been some result or change in that area that could indicate the gwyllion's presence. If a gwyllion follows you home and takes up residence in your house, and you then move, leave a small silver coin or penny behind to let him know he has not been abandoned.

HEARTHFAY

ABOVE *Leave a tiny plate of food in the hearthfay's home and watch it vanish!*

Hearthfays are distant cousins of house brownies and similar in appearance, being small and of dark brown and purple coloring. The hearthfay has burning red or yellow eyes and, although a squat little figure overall, he or she does have unusually long and spindly fingers and toes. Their hair, also long, is dark, glossy, and straight, and they all like to wear fringes half covering their eyes. Hearthfays have delicate, feathery wings. These are usually folded across their backs unless they have become emotional in some way, when they will spread their wings to the maximum ability (their way of looking fierce). The hearthfay sits at the back of the fireplace and has a lot in common with salamanders, being attracted to very warm places. The one notable facet of a hearthfay's personality is its deep shyness. If you look directly at a hearthfay, he or she will usually vanish

immediately. It prefers to skulk at the back of the dark, warm fireplace and stare at you. But a hearthfay also cares for you and your wellbeing so as long as you acknowledge its presence gently and go about your household as normal, you'll find in time it will watch over you when you turn to grab the kettle or open the oven door.

Hearthfays prefer to live in original fireplaces or hearths, but with the introduction of central heating and modern homes, they have migrated further to live in any suitable dark corner of the house, including cookers. In one instance, I heard about a hearthfay that had become very attached to the top of a microwave oven. In days gone by, almost every home had a hearth and most hearths housed a fairy. The fireplace hearth was the heart and soul of the home: it provided heat for warmth, for cooking, for heating water, and

was a comfortable place to huddle around during winter when the weather would howl and beat against the door. In those times the hearthfay's job was usually to keep an eye on pots boiling over and birds falling down chimneys, but nowadays, if you get to know your hearthfay well, you may find he or she ventures further out and takes an interest in your broken toaster or coffee machine. In ancient Roman times, the hearth was believed to be the domain of all the domestic gods, and rituals were performed in order to keep this

TO CATCH A HEARTHFAY

Hearthfays are attracted to baking smells and a house with a well-used kitchen. A freshly cooked apple pie, loaf of bread, or fruit cake will create the kind of smell the hearthfay adores, and if left next to your fireplace or on an open windowsill can be a powerful incentive to move in. If you do not have a fireplace hearth, look in your home for a warm and dark nook or cranny that might appeal to a hearthfay. If you really do not have anywhere suitable, you could make a little shaded corner—perhaps a table with a cloth over it—but this is not ideal, because hearthfays usually look for permanent structures to dwell in. Having found your dark nook, make a little shrine to the hearthfay. This should consist of a small bunch of mint in a glass containing a mixture of baking soda and water (they adore the smell of mint and the soda bubbles). Also, leave an acorn cup filled with dew and a little heap of ash or a lump of coal (this will make them feel particularly at home). Every night for seven days in a row, when the house is asleep, sing this song very quietly to the hearthfay:

> Little hearthfay look this way,
>> I have built a place to stay,
> Little hearthfay hear my song,
>> Welcome here both safe and long.

Keep your eye on the chosen area and make a note if any of the objects have moved at all—this will be your first indication that a hearthfay is interested in moving in. Remember, they are notoriously shy, so even if you do see a wisp of a movement out of the corner of your eye, try not to react; the hearthfay will gradually feel more confident about being there and should slowly reveal itself to you. The only successful way to keep a hearthfay is to ensure that your home, and, in particular, your kitchen is kept cheerful, warm, and comforting. Once you sense the hearthfay's presence, chat to it regularly and, even if you haven't seen it yet, always address the nook or corner you have chosen.

place special and sacred. The hearth was always kept scrupulously clean and often left burning overnight to ensure the approval of the spirits it contained. Often, when families moved home, they would take a piece of the burning hearth fire with them to start a new fire in their new hearth and thus transfer their own particular Fay with them to the new home. This is where the idea and title of a "housewarming" party comes from.

Traditional ways to communicate with a hearthfay usually center around the hearth and cleaning. If you wash the hearth with a solution of elder leaves and boiled water, it will give off a special scent to the fairy and indicate that she is welcome in your home. Hanging dried hawthorn over the fireplace pleases hearthfays as they use the leaves in their own magick works. Walnut shells are always welcomed as a means of barter and finance. They are useful to all the fairies in many ways, making perfect baby carriages, for example.

RIGHT *The smell of newly baked bread is a favorite of the little hearthfay.*

HOBGOBLIN

RIGHT *Hobgoblins sometimes have mood swings so do treat them kindly.*

Also known as boggarts, hobgoblins are mischievous creatures, who adore the humans that they often play tricks on. The hobgoblin is also happy to help around the home; however, he will more likely be found sweeping the dust under the carpet than off it. Hobgoblins are often seen carrying brooms: these are used to fly about on, swat flies with, and for other non-domestic purposes. Like the satyr, the hobgoblin is half-human, having horns on his head and goatlike thick, curly hair on both head and legs. The hobgoblin is a fertility spirit with the power to change shape, and one of the most famous hobgoblins of all was Robin Goodfellow, also known as Puck. Hobgoblins love a good party and will be found anywhere there is a plentiful supply of food, drink, and music. Playing tricks is their trademark, but they are not ever meant nastily.

TO CATCH A HOBGOBLIN

Hold a big party in an outside area and lay an extra place to one side of the main table. Put a large glass of beer there and then contain the setting and beer within a boundary of cowrie shells, ivy, holly, and tobacco leaves. This will attract the hobgoblin. As the party gets merrier, keep checking the hobgoblin's place and talk to him. Come and go and speak cheerfully whenever you address him. If you are true in spirit, he will know it and your friendship will begin. Never forget when partying in the future to always lay a place for your hobgoblin friend—if you forget him, he will also forget you, despite your good times together.

I was told by a great-aunt that if you hang a circlet of holly outside your door, you will stop a hobgoblin from entering because he will stay outside and try to count the holly berries, even if there are none! On the roofs of some very old houses you can often see a small ledge near the base of the chimney. This was known as the "goblin's seat." It was built into the chimney to give a resting place for these fairy folk, rather than inviting them in.

IMP

RIGHT *Not mischievous by nature, imps often remove paperwork for their own use.*

Great friends of witches, imps are usually invisible, but if you are lucky enough to see one, you are advised to catch it immediately and keep it in a small bottle with a tiny amount of fresh water at the bottom, securely sealed with a cork. The imp is very happy living in the essence of the water within the bottle and after about a week will come to regard it as his home, when you can let him out and be certain he will return to it regularly. Tiny and human-like in appearance, but completely hairless, imps have a great fondness for opulent clothes, with a penchant for velvet cloaks and furry hats. They also wear belts with many items, such as scissors, pens, and pencils hanging from them. Their chief duties are administration of all sorts, but magick most of all. When you lose papers that you are certain were left exactly in one place, the imp will find them for you.

TO CATCH AN IMP

Take an empty bottle with a cork and fill the bottom with a little warm water and a hazelnut. Leave it on your window sill, preferably behind a drape. In front of the bottle, leave a tiny trail of tobacco leading up to and into the bottle. Before going to bed, whisper very quietly in front of the bottle the magick words, "Io, zati, zata, abata." These words will hang in the air in front of the bottle, drawing the imp to them. In the morning, check your bottle. If there is anything disturbed or unusual in it, quickly cork it up. You have caught your imp. Now you must leave him there for a week, after which let him out. Remember that he is often invisible, so don't be fooled into letting him go just because you can't see him.

(Although not mischievous by nature, it may have been the imp that removed them in the first place.)

If an imp does seem to be disturbing your paperwork rather a lot, a good deflection spell is to hang a rowan twig tied with a white ribbon above your desk. It creates a mystical barrier that stops the little imp from interfering! An iron horseshoe hung, points down, also creates a similar barrier by containing all the goodness inside the semicircle and not letting anything get past.

K ELPIE

RIGHT *Watching the foaming waves of the sea, you may just see a kelpie ride.*

Very fierce water spirits, who are inclined to take the shape of horses or horses with human heads, kelpies can often be seen when the sea is rough and they ride along the edges of large waves. They are relatives of Macha, Rhiannon, and Epona the Horse Goddess (who has a horse's body with a female head and is guardian of the dead and those in danger). These three are representations of the cosmic goddess as triple goddess: Macha is the Irish name, Rhiannon is the Welsh name, and Epona is the Roman name. Epona carries the keys to the Otherworld and opens the door for those souls passing through to the other side. Kelpies help to pull the boats containing the souls bound for the underworld. These boats start off on top of the water and then sink below to continue their journey. If you anger a kelpie, it will take you to the deepest part of the ocean and drown you.

TO CATCH A KELPIE

Ride a horse barefooted, along the beach, letting your hair flow free and your spirit soar with the waves. The minute you let go of the cares of earthly awareness and connect with the spirit of the sea, the kelpie will hear you and may join you in your ride. Stop your horse, dismount, and walk back the way you came, putting your bare feet in the marks left by your horse and the invisible kelpie. You are now metaphysically attaching yourself to the kelpie, and from now on the horse that you rode will have the spirit of the kelpie at its side whenever you ride together again, and will be sure to bring its own wild magick into your life.

LEPRECHAUN

Leprechauns are known all over the world by various indigenous names. These refer to the same fairy with the same traits, however, and the most commonly known is the Irish leprechaun, or clocharachan. They live mostly underground because they are fairies of the Earth. You can also find them in boggy marshes, caves, and some damp basement apartments. Their job is fairy shoemaker or cobbler. Leprechauns are very wealthy because all the buried treasure in the Earth is owned by them. As relatives of dwarfs and gnomes, they usually look similar to tiny, wizened old men, about 3½ inches high with strangely long and pointed noses, wearing Earth colors such as green, red, and brown, and they are also very fond of hats. They traditionally wear breeches, suspenders, and waistcoats. Their boots have shiny buckles on them and the end of the boots have a

TO CATCH A LEPRECHAUN

Take a good bunch of ragwort and either a shiny silver or gold coin, or a miniature tool that could be used by the leprechaun. Leave the gift under the ragwort at the opening of a cave or the foot of a hill, and then hide nearby. When the leprechaun comes along, because of his attraction to the ragwort, he will immediately go there and start investigating his find. You must quickly jump out and grab his purse or hat. Once you have those, the leprechaun will not leave your side. Although he owns all the gold in the ground, the leprechaun cannot ever give anything away unless he wants to; so as long as you have his hat or purse, he will follow you everywhere.

BELOW *If a leprechaun can't
get his purse, he won't go and
your money won't either!*

propensity to turn upward. They like bright, shiny buttons on their jackets and always carry a purse or bag filled with gold and silver. Although very fond of their wealth, they are known to be especially helpful to the poor and will often leave money lying around on the ground for them to find. They are very hard to catch, and if you do have the good fortune to catch a leprechaun, do not trust a word he says. He will do anything to escape. The minute you stop looking at him, he'll be gone. However, it's worth trying to catch a leprechaun because he can help you financially. Traditionally, you should always ask a leprechaun where he keeps his crock of gold. However, if you catch a leprechaun and keep him in your house, then you will never be short of money. Leprechauns are best found in hills, bogs, and caves at the beginning of the day.

MERMAID AND MERMAN

Mermaids and mermen live under the sea in beautiful sunken palaces decorated with the contents of shipwrecks. Associated with the moon, they are rulers of the tides and followers of the beauty and treachery of the sea. Friends of all the creatures within the sea, these are very ancient fairies with soft, white human-like upper bodies and tails like fish, and there have been many reported sightings of them in the past. They ride dolphins and eels and collect the souls of drowned mortals. Although they can both change into human form, mermen prefer to stay underwater and very rarely leave their Otherworld homes. If they do, it is usually for one of two reasons—either to meet with selkies and row the fairy barges across the water or to fight. So it is debatable whether you would be fortunate or not if you should come across a merman. Mermaids, on the other hand, like to sit out of the sea on small, secluded rocks, combing their beautiful hair and singing. Mermaids have silvery white skin and salmon-like tails with shiny scales, purple, blue or green eyes, and long, flowing blonde or green hair. They carry silver combs and mirrors and wear seaweed fronds and tinkling, pale-colored shell belts for adornment. They also have tiny sealskin hats, which they use when changing form. The mermaid is helpless without her cap because she is then forced to remain on land.

Mermen have different tails, which are smooth and speckled like a porpoise with no scales. However, they do have long bristles attached to the side of their head and reaching to their shoulders, which they can raise and lower like a crest when they get

RIGHT *Mermaids are traditionally very beautiful fairy folk.*

angry. They are very good-looking and
traditionally have long, black beards and
very dark, almost black eyes. Both mermaids
and mermen have webbed fingers and, when
in mortal form, webbed toes. Merpeople have
a strange, chanting language, which is
normally spoken by the mermaid since
mermen are reticent by nature and prefer to
keep silent. Although mermen are wary of
humans, the mermaid believes it is her duty
to warn mortals of approaching dangers such
as sea storms, oil spills, and shipwrecks.

Mermaids have very big hearts and are
very fond of humans because they are the
bewitching descendants of the siren and
ancient fin folk, and as such, they understand
the attractions of the human life. It is for this
reason that, although bound to the sea, a
mermaid will have no hesitation in seeking
out and joining in with the fun of a human
party for a while!

TO CATCH A MERPERSON

As with a fairshee, to catch a merperson you must first make it fall in love with you. Fishermen and sea folk stand the most chance because they have a lot in common with these fairies. However, I believe everyone should try at least once. There are various famous places in Britain said to be the haunts of merpeople, for example, a Cave called Piper's Hole on the Scilly Isle of Tresco, or Mermaid's Rock, in East Cornwall, or the Doom Bar sandbar in Padstow Harbour. Local people may tell you more if you inquire carefully. If you can, go to one of these enchanted places (otherwise, any rocky inlet by the sea will do), and look out for anyone swimming around a lot or sitting on the rocks, singing. Hang a bunch of dried seaweed on the rocks and place a little net sprinkled with rock salt on the water as offerings. You could also throw a small, brightly painted wooden fish into the water as a gift. Don't forget that merpeople can change tails to legs and back again in a second, so be absolutely sure it's a merperson you are trying to woo and not a merry holiday-maker, or you might get into trouble! Now it's up to you to use your charm. Having attracted it to you, steal the merperson's shell belt or little sealskin hat, and it will be spellbound to you forever, or at least until you give its belongings back. You must always remember that merpeople have very big hearts—it is essential that you don't hurt their feelings. After all, the last thing you want is to stir up a storm at sea!

RIGHT The fairy water folk visit certain enchanted places.

NYMPH

Nymph is a collective term for the witch-
fairies descended from pre-Christian pagan
priestesses, mostly female in spirit. They are
connected either with sacred water areas
and known as *latis*, which means Goddess of
the Pool, or connected to sacred groves and
known as *ratis*, which means Goddess of the
Fortress. The name "nymph" means "nubile
maiden," and nymphs are associated with
healing and fertility. According to tradition,
drinking the waters where nymphs live is
supposed to make you fertile, and because
of this the waters are referred to as the
fountains of life. You can make a special
offering by dipping the petals of white or
yellow chrysanthemums in whiskey. There are
many natural shrines in wooded groves and
water areas around the world and these are
the places to make your prayers or leave
offerings in order to communicate with

TO CATCH A NYMPH

*A nymph will come with you willingly
if she senses your deep need and honest
spirit; otherwise, she will stay where she
prefers to be and simply reveal herself
from time to time. Should you have
particular need of her, simply go to a
natural shrine and hang a piece of your
clothing on the trees or around the
water's edge of your chosen shrine.
Speak to the nymph, pouring out your
troubles or desires. Then, kiss the
ground and turn around three times
counterclockwise and go home. Do not,
ever, look behind you as you go. If your
needs are not in some way answered
within one week, return to the site and
keep talking.*

nymphs. Famous nymphs include Arnemetia of Buxton; Sul of Bath; Boand of the River Boyne; Nantosvelta of the winding streams; Flidais; and Coventina. Most of the time they remain invisible, although they can be seen if you stay quiet for long enough, and nymphs will assume human appearance when they need to accomplish something. They accept white stones as offerings, particularly with regard to magick concerned with the weather.

PISKY (PIXIE)

Piskies are a type of fairy found predominantly in Cornwall, England, and are wel-known as the Cornish Pixie. Piskies are great friends with spriggans, who are also indigenous to Cornwall. The spriggan is a frightening giant spirit, who can change shape at will and whose main purpose in life is to guard ancient treasures that lie hidden beneath prehistoric Standing Stones. Piskies live around the edges of prehistoric Standing Stones, both below and above ground. They have two main sets of clothes: their everyday apparel, which is usually green with a scarlet cap, and their best clothes, which are a scarlet coat and black steeple-crowned hat. They are famous for mazing humans, which means that when mortals are walking on familiar paths, the pisky comes along and, by magick, mazes them so that they lose their way. No matter how well known the path or

TO CATCH A PISKY

Visit a Standing Stone if you can. Take off your jacket, turn it inside out, and then put it on again. You have now mazed the pisky and, by entering his world, you have instinctively attracted him to you. Now sit quietly with your back against the Standing Stone and explain why you need a pisky in your life—and it had better be a good reason. If you think you've been stung or feel ill in any way, say goodbye to the pisky immediately and turn your jacket back the right way. If you feel that you are communing successfully, take a coin out of your pocket and place it on the ground in front of you. Say out loud that this is the pisky's payment for the first year's service if he is willing.

BELOW *When a pisky gets
angry, he will sometimes
throw a burning stone at you.*

countryside may be, when you have been
mazed, you will lose all sense of direction.
The remedy for this is to simply take off a
piece of your clothing, such as your jacket,
and turn it inside out. The reason why this
will work is because the pisky has turned the
atmospheric ether around you inside out, so if
you turn a piece of your clothing (which is
physically attuned to you) inside out as well,
the two will be balanced and everything will
return to normal. Mostly clean shaven with
bright red cheeks, piskies favor long, wispy
beards as they get older. They are very good
fighters when they need to be and, when
angry, like to throw pebbles that have been
heated in fire (known as burning stones) or
use spears, bows and arrows, or catapults.
However, when successfully caught or made
friends with, a pisky will become your
defender and personal guardian.

POOKA

At my grandmother's house in Norfolk, England, I once inadvertently rode a pooka when I was about 11 years old. My sister and I had gone to a nearby farm to ride their horses and I had chosen a very large, very black horse. After I had been helped onto his back, the horse suddenly took off with the speed of the wind beneath his feet. It was all I could do just to cling onto his silky mane, so fast were we going. The pooka (if that is what he was, and I have no reason to doubt it) flew into a nearby forest and up to the edge of a quarry. By this time, being extremely frightened, I started screaming prayers to the Green Man for help. Suddenly, just before the extreme edge of the quarry, the pooka dug his hooves into the crumbling floor and put his neck down. I went flying over his head and landed upside down on the very edge of the quarry. Luckily, I was not particularly hurt and

remained winded and lying on the ground while my equine friend raced off into the distance. Shortly afterward my sister appeared on the back of a brown mare and seemed somewhat surprised to find me sitting alone. I briefly explained what had happened and we returned to the farm to make absolutely sure the pooka spirit had returned the horse. Nothing can ever make me forget that frightening and yet exhilarating ride, and to my mind it was the perfect example of a pooka scare. A pooka takes on the shape of various animals, but favors the horse, in order to race around the Earth. They are very mischievous fairies and specifically enjoy catching humans on their backs and taking them for long, frightening rides through

RIGHT *Pookas are mischievous by nature and dislike being caught.*

forests and up mountains. In their human guise, pookas have very sharp features and the most amazing huge eyes, with leathery batlike wings folded tightly over their shoulders. However, typically, they mostly appear in animal form. Traditionally, they are fairy messengers but because of their naughty nature, they like to play tricks on humans as they deliver their messages. They look out for anyone lost or tired and then appear as a horse, dog, goat, bull, donkey, or combination of animals. If you get on its back, it will race like the wind and do its very

ABOVE *The rapid ride of a pooka often emulates a rapid success in your life.*

best to scare you witless! According to custom, they live mostly in the Otherworld and visit this world only during the sabbat festivals, when fairies and humans pass easily between the two worlds. Their favorite visiting times are Beltain (Cetshamain), the evening of May 1–2 and Samhain (Halloween) the evening of October 31–November 1. Catching a pooka guarantees safe travel, and swift communication in your life.

TO CATCH A POOKA

A pooka will often appear if you crush a St. John's wort plant underfoot. The plant is sacred to them, so if it is harmed in any way, even by accident, the pooka will be at your side in a moment. However, if you crush the plant on purpose, you will be disliked by the pooka and ultimately are simply asking to be ignored. The best thing to do if you want to catch a pooka is to wait until the eve of one of the sabbats, and sit by the side of a road or path until the pooka appears. If an animal suddenly does materialize out of the dusk, try and ride it. If it gallops off, you almost certainly are having a pooka ride. It will be fast and furious and scare you to bits. The pooka usually stops only at daybreak or dawn and that is when you have to try and stay on him in order to catch him. The pooka will obviously try and return to the Otherworld, but in order to keep him, you must tame him and stay on his back. This is not easy. If you

have tamed a pooka and ridden him home, he will change back into human form and you can keep him only until the same evening. After this time he will change back into animal form and ride off again. To stop the pooka from escaping into the night, you have to ride him each subsequent day until past the daybreak hour, again and again. As you can imagine, this is incredibly tiring and the pooka will never stop trying to escape. So if you have the rather questionable good fortune to catch a pooka, use that fortune wisely for one day and then let him go.

$\mathcal{S}$ ALAMANDER

RIGHT *Wherever there is
a fire there will be a
salamander waiting.*

This elemental spirit of fire is larger than the firefays and is usually between about $1/2$ – 2 inches long. A combination of red, yellow, and orange in color and initially dragonlike, with long, thin tails and wide, stretching wings, the salamander has evolved into a more humanlike appearance, but retains the lizard-like features, curling tail, and scaly skin. Salamanders dwell in fire and love the heat. They die when the fire or candle they live in is extinguished, but they are immediately reborn when the fire or candle is relit. If you stare long enough into the flame of a candle or fire, you should eventually see the salamander, which will grow, stretch, and diminish in a never-ending cycle of flaming wonder in front of your eyes. If you ever have difficulties in lighting a fire or a candle, the reason is probably that the salamander is in a bad mood! If anything falls from the flames in

TO CATCH
A SALAMANDER

Because a salamander is an elemental, it will be constantly present in any form of fire, such as a fireplace or candle; so in order to catch one all you need to do is light a candle. However, if you need the particular help of a salamander, light a fire or a candle and take a bundle of ash twigs and tie them with a wet, green twig. Throw the bundle in the fire or hold it carefully over the candle flame, and when the twigs start to snap and crackle, make a wish to the salamander for what you need. Witches often ask for the help of salamanders when they want to raise a storm at sea, by using a spell that incorporates throwing eggshells into the domain of the salamander's fire.

front of you, such as soot or candle wax, this is a message from the salamander— someone is on their way to visit and you should extinguish the fire! To cleanse the fireplace or candle holder and give a sweet scent for the salamander's home, you should burn rosemary and angelica leaves. To seek the help of a salamander in finding a lover, hang a crab-apple tied with red cotton over the salamander's flames. If the apple falls from the cotton, it means the salamander will be on your case!

SELKIE

RIGHT *Selkies have webbed fingers and horny skin on the soles of their feet.*

Sweet, large, and indolent water fairies who appear in the shape of seals, selkies are often found basking around the edges of the coastline. It is believed, though, that their official places of origin are a tiny, secret island off the North Norfolk coast and a rocky inlet to the west of the Orkney Islands. In mortal form they have big brown and gold-flecked eyes, and range in speckled skin tones from pale cream to cookie color. Usually they assume human form at nighttime by casting off their coats, although they prefer to resume seal form by the first light of day. If you steal its discarded coat, you will have a selkie in your power and it will have to stay with you until it can regain its seal coat. Guardians of the fairy loaf—a small, round fossilized sea urchin, about 70 million years old and known as an echinite—the selkie can help you with magick from this fairy loaf. Selkies are both

TO CATCH A SELKIE

Selkies swim extremely well and fast, but the best way to catch one is when it is just lazily floating about on top of the water, which it does rather a lot in both human and seal form. You really need a boat to catch a selkie because of their quickness in the water once they know you've spotted them. Their favorite food, whatever form they have chosen, is chopped liver and salmon. If you keep very quiet in a bobbing boat and scatter the food on top of the water, you are bound to soon hear the splish splosh of a lazy selkie coming to investigate. My Uncle Pattick is very fond of selkies and often takes his boat out to visit them. Only if a selkie discards its coat by itself at nighttime can you keep it.

male and female. Originally they were said to be humans who were put under a spell that transformed them into seals. Because of the spell, the very first selkies could resume human form once a year only, on Midsummer's Eve, when they would cast off their coats and dance upon the shore. However, modern descendants of selkie and human marriages can now choose when they change shape.

$\int$ IREN AND HARPY

RIGHT *Sirens and harpies are known as "sisters of strife."*

Sirens and harpies are sisters. Both have female upper bodies and birdlike lower bodies. Sirens are the water spirits of ancient times and harpies are the air spirits. Sirens are best known to sit in meadows by the sea, singing enchanted songs that lure mortal men to their doom. They are known as "calmers of the wind," but despite this attractive name are extremely dangerous. They are both very fond of female humans, but unfortunately, sirens and harpies do not like male humans at all and any man would be well advised to steer clear from either fairy. Sailors would often hear the song of the siren and swim ashore to investigate, whereupon they would perish in some form or other most miserably. The only way to ignore a siren is for the mortal male to stuff his ears with absorbent cotton or something similar and never look her way. Sirens have been known to sit on piles of male human bones, which have been enchanted to look like soft, grassy hills. Over time, and particularly recorded in the Middle Ages, the siren's form changed and she lost her lower bird body to be replaced by a fish tail, whereupon she joined her sisters and brothers in the mer-palaces under the sea. However, the siren's anger toward the male species never abated, so be warned. As far as female humans are concerned, sirens can be their best friends, protecting them at all costs and loading them with food and plenty.

Famous sirens of the past include Thelxiope (enchanting face), Molpe (musical), and Aglaophonus (lovely voice). The ancient Greeks and Romans believed that sirens became loving and gentle after their deaths and decorated shrines in their honor.

Harpies are also upper-half female and lower-half bird in form, and are connected

with the air and wind. The harpy is associated with storms and whirlwinds and is known to carry away wrongdoers in its claws and take them to the furies for punishment. Famous harpies of the past include: Podarge (swift foot), Aello (storm wind), Ocypete (swift flyer), Nicothoe (victorious speed), and Aellopus (wind foot). Harpies are still not overly fond of male humans, but will lavish the female human with all she requires. Harpies are sometimes known as "snatchers of men," and as such are regarded as rather dangerous.

Phorcys is the father of sirens and harpies and is a very virile sea god, who is strongly protective of his female bird daughters. I wouldn't really recommend trying to catch either a siren or a harpy, unless you are a strong female who requires a very strong

TO CATCH A SIREN OR A HARPY

Hang around the seaside, whistling and singing as you walk along the seashore. If you're male, prepare to meet your doom; if you're female, take particular notice of any other females or birds that approach or follow you. In these modern days, sirens and harpies affect many disguises. Once you feel you may have the attention of one of these mystic creatures, make a wish out loud and then blow it over the sea and onto the wind. Depending on whether you've caught a siren or harpy, your life should suddenly become strangely enriched by the appearance of birds, wind, or water references. What you make of this magick is between you and your mystical sister.

ABOVE *Sirens have now gone back to the sea, but once flew with their harpy cousin.*

female counterpart—and if you are a male, forget it. If you are in the position of having a harpy or siren attracted to you, handle them with care! They are used to a fine way of life and can be unwittingly arrogant and quick-tempered as a result of this upbringing. However, if you know how to treat them well, you can be assured of having fine times and luxurious, unexpected gifts dropping into your life now and again from this rare sisterhood of fairy bird-women.

SYLPH

RIGHT *Sylphs are so delicate they are easily missed when standing still.*

These elemental spirits of air are also known as astral fairies, since they ride on the back of the wind. Sylphs are extremely tall female fairies, around 8–10 feet in height and uncommonly slender and slim. They are also extremely beautiful fairies, who have many pulsating ribbons of colored light emanating from them, which are part of their wing structure. Sylphs are also partly transparent, which enhances the enchanting otherworldliness of their appearance. A sylph is a great fairy to have around you for metaphysical purposes—if you are at all interested in matters of mind, body and spirit, a sylph is the best teacher to help you in your work. It is not easy to catch a sylph, but if you succeed in attracting one to you, she will protect you from all harm and, with her pulsating lights, will help your wishes to enter the ethereal stream.

TO CATCH A SYLPH

In order to attract their attention, you should practice "whistling up the wind" to get sylphs to notice you. Whistling gently in tune calls the wind and the fairies to you by sympathetic magick. Certain types of incense, such as jasmine, sandalwood, and patchouli, also attract sylphs. Like sirens and harpies, you can make one wish out loud to the sylphs. However, unlike the bird-women who live near the sea, sylphs can be whistled to anywhere. Catching a sylph takes practice and there is no way you can keep her for good. Be content with calling her whenever you need her advice or spiritual strength.

TROLL

Originally indigenous to Scandinavia, the troll, like the undine, can now be found all over the modern world. Trolls live in fairly large family units with a king and queen overseeing each area's group. They are little people ranging in height up to a maximum of 3 feet, and usually described as ugly. However, although they don't have the traditional smooth-faced beauty of fairies like the undine/nixie or flowerfay, the troll has its own kind of earthy and Otherworldly strangeness, which can certainly be called beautiful in its own way. With long, straight, thick hair ranging in all the colors of nature, thick-set bodies, and large, fleshy noses and ears, the troll can be confidently said to have a style all of its own. Both male and female

RIGHT *Trolls are very wise,*
but prefer to keep their
knowledge to themselves.

TO CATCH A TROLL

Go to a mountainous or wooded area and make a little fire. Throw onto it a handful of coltsfoot herb. Say these magick words, "Paganus Larva, fictus fabulosus, apparere conspici, Statim! Confestim! Extemplo!" Now take a hair from your head and throw it into the fire. If you hear any tiny noises behind you (and they are not obviously something dangerous), keep very still, watching the fire until it burns low. You have communicated spiritually and metaphysically with the trolls and your life should begin on its newly acquired troll-enhanced path.

trolls like smoking tiny clay or wood pipes of coltsfoot herb. Not very fond of clothes, they are, however, extremely keen on wearing stripy stockings. Their preference for stout boots is mainly due to the fact that they hate getting their feet wet. Trolls have been maligned in the past and wrongly credited with evildoing and sometimes even with eating human flesh. Nothing could be further from the truth. As in all communities, trolls have their fair share of black sheep and are in no way different from any other tribe. However, like gnomes, trolls are Earth fairies, and holders of great wisdom and knowledge. They are known to have quick tempers, but I believe the worst a troll would do if you insulted it, is to shout loudly or to stamp its feet before disappearing into the Earth. They might sulk for a little while after that, but not for long.

UNDINE (NIXIE) AND NAIAD

Elemental spirit of water, undines (or nixies as they are known in some places, including Germany), are very beautiful freshwater fairies, seen all over the world, with oval faces, long yellow or green hair, and wide, yellow or green eyes. They are very strong and in appearance are tall and slim, having a strange skin color combination of gray and white with an intense silver sheen; the skin itself is damp to the touch. Their wings are as fine as cobwebs but, paradoxically, are also immensely strong. They carry little lacey bags of pale magick pebbles and if you ever find one of these pebbles, it will bring you immeasurable luck. Their clothes (when they wear them) are usually transparent and lacey, and they have a particular love of frilly edgings around necks, sleeves, and hems, which I believe reflects their love of foaming water. Undines love singing and brushing

their hair and they look out for humans that may be in trouble in the water. Because of an ancient promise, undines have to save at least one drowned human soul per year. They keep these souls in small upturned earthenware pots buried at the bottom of the water, and the human soul can return to Earth for a visit once a year at Samhain (Halloween). You can often see undines if you are whitewater-rafting, for example, as one of their favorite games is to chase the boats. Their usual home is beneath waterfalls and other fast-moving water. Apart from that, ancient Germanic lore tells of undines that would transform themselves into old women and walk on land to the local markets, where they would marvel at all the fresh fruit and vegetables.

RIGHT *The undine is a very feminine fairy and loves to play in water.*

TO CATCH AN UNDINE/NIXIE

Attempt to catch an undine only if you have somewhere suitable to offer her as a home, such as a nearby pool or naturally occurring waterfall. You might be able to successfully keep an undine in your shower if she loves you enough, but keep an eye on your household water consumption. Firstly, take her a gift of waterlilies and throw them in the watery place you feel she may be. If the lilies sink or disappear, this is a sign that she has accepted your gift. Now sit at the edge of the water and softly sing a few verses of your favorite song until you have caught her attention. Whisper to her about why you would like her to move to your home and explain that she would be free to do as she pleases (undines are one of the most independent of the fairy folk). If you sense agreement on her part, now

is the time to return home and await her arrival. Being fiercely independent, the undine will make her own way to your home. Have no fear, you will be clearly aware that an undine has decided to live near you—anything to do with water will soon, inevitably, be drawn to your attention. This has its downsides too, since you may become aware of liquids spilling or water mains and pipes exploding more often in your home than before. Places that suffer from habitual flooding are often inhabited by a collection of undines (and therefore rather too many). So you might like to check with your neighbors first before inviting one back to stay with you.

If you ever want an undine to leave, simply get rid of any water features and she will disappear in a splash to search for damper climes.

The naiad is a cousin of the undine, who shares many similarities to the undine. However, the naiad prefers living in calmer places, such as the bottom of rivers and lakes. Unfortunately, the naiad is well known for her speciality, which is to drown humans. She lures humans out to the middle of rivers or lakes and then does everything she can to capsize their boats or tire them out and make sure they drown. Equally unfortunately, for humans, the naiad is extraordinarily pretty, which is one of the lures she uses to get humans to come after her. Naiads have dark-green or blue hair, pale-colored eyes, and very pointed chins. Their fingers and toes are long and slim but the hands and feet are webbed in between. Naiads will never come out on land and, bearing in mind their nasty behavior toward humans, there is absolutely no point whatsoever in trying to catch them.

ISKIE

Wiskies are teeny, weeny little fairies, black in color and with silver wings, and are prolific in number within the confines of dark, damp, and sweet-smelling woods. The best places to look for wiskies are in dark, wooded areas and forests. They are seen quite clearly when patches of sunlight stream through the tree tops and create pure shafts of light descending to the forest floor. Within that shaft, if you look carefully enough, you will see many wiskies dancing and tumbling through the air. In these modern days, they can also be found in places such as the light shafts that stream through the broken glass windows often found in greenhouses. However, this is rare, due to the surrounding light of the greenhouse being too strong. If you find a dark place with a pure shaft of sunlight, you are bound to see wiskies dancing. Look at the light shaft carefully,

TO CATCH A WISKIE

This method of catching wiskies was given to me by my dear Aunty Mary (who is actually part garden-fairy), and she says that this is the best way to catch wiskies, but you must always put them back when you've had a good look at and chat with them. Wiskies cannot be kept indefinitely; they would pine and probably wink out of existence if you took them away from their beloved woods. Aunty Mary says to take a tiny pot of honey and go into the woods where wild orchids grow. Place a little smear of honey on the orchid's petals and hide nearby. The smell of orchid and honey is irresistible to wiskies and soon, if you wait long enough, they will fly down and get stuck in the honey. Then you can help them out of it.

close your eyes tightly for a few seconds, and then look again. Wiskies are about $1/16$ inch high and look like miniscule humans with weeny, staring, catlike, silver eyes. Neither are noticeably male or female, but if you look

carefully, the male wiskie usually has a tiny crest-like ruff around his neck. They are traditionally messenger fairies between this and the Otherworld— if you have a special message, stand under a wiskie light shaft.